HORTICULTURE
FOR THE DISABLED
AND DISADVANTAGED

HORTICULTURE FOR THE DISABLED AND DISADVANTAGED

By

DAMON R. OLSZOWY, Ph.D.

CHARLES C THOMAS • PUBLISHER

Springfield • Illinois • U.S.A.

Published and Distributed Throughout the World by
CHARLES C THOMAS • PUBLISHER
Bannerstone House
301-327 East Lawrence Avenue, Springfield, Illinois, U.S.A.

© *1978, by* CHARLES C THOMAS • PUBLISHER

ISBN 0-398-03691-8

Library of Congress Catalog Card Number: 77-8390

With THOMAS BOOKS *careful attention is given to all details of
manufacturing and design. It is the Publisher's desire to present books that
are satisfactory as to their physical qualities and artistic possibilities and
appropriate for their particular use.* THOMAS BOOKS *will be true to those
laws of quality that assure a good name and good will.*

Printed in the United States of America
OO-2

Library of Congress Cataloging in Publication Data

Olszowy, Damon R
   Horticulture for the disabled and disadvantaged.

   Bibliography: p.
   Includes index.
   1. Gardening--Therapeutic use. I. Title.
[DNLM: 1. Occupational therapy. 2. Plants.
3. Rehabilitation. WB555 052]
RM735.7.G37047   615'.8515   77-8390
ISBN 0-398-03691-8

PREFACE

Two hundred years ago, Americans were granted "life, liberty and the pursuit of happiness." For the disabled and disadvantaged of our society, the ability to participate with dignity in the activities of everyday living and to take advantage of their "inalienable rights" is just beginning to be realized. Today, there are an estimated 50 million Americans that have some physical impairment. With about 444,000 new cases of stroke alone occurring each year, it is predicted that, by 1980, for every able-bodied individual, there will be one person with a physical disability, chronic or otherwise.

Moving into its third century, our country turns its focus, not on the accomplishments of the past, but on the factors compelling a new response to meet the needs of those who are disabled and disadvantaged. Great progress has been made in the treatment of many individuals. Special services and innovative programs are being developed to meet their needs. In general, there is a more enlightened sense of equity with respect to minorities.

One such innovative approach is the use of horticulture for therapy and rehabilitation. Horticulture has been employed both experimentally and casually over the years; however, only recently has it been acknowledged and appreciated as a therapeutic and rehabilitative medium. There does exist a large body of relevant information and knowledge, and also a set of principles that makes horticultural therapy a distinct discipline. Therefore, there is a need for a comprehensive text that sets down these principles, and also that provides guidelines and up-to-date information to individuals, groups, and institutions who plan to establish a horticultural program.

The observations, methods, and activities described in this book were used in a pilot program conducted by the Bartlett

Arboretum of the University of Connecticut (UCONN) in cooperation with the Easter Seal Rehabilitation Center of Southwestern Connecticut (ESRCSC). The Connecticut Commission for Higher Education provided a community service grant to help support the program under Title I HEA.

Observations made by staff members of the ESRCSC during the physical restoration phase of patient admission and through periodic follow-up after discharge indicated that non-involvement, inability to return to gainful employment, and lack of purposeful daily activities were some of the major negative characteristics of the present rehabilitative process. Institutions have long recognized these problems and are striving to lessen them through horticulture. This was reflected in a nationwide survey conducted in 1968 by the Menninger Foundation in which 64 percent of the 216 hospitals responding to a questionnaire reported that they had some kind of garden or greenhouse program. The Menninger Clinic has for many years used garden therapy in the rehabilitative process. New York University Medical Center's Institute of Rehabilitation Medicine has enjoyed the use of a therapeutic greenhouse since 1959 in which patients find joy and solace and learn to live with dignity and independence.

Many existing therapeutic communities for the disabled and disadvantaged are limited to physical restoration, and there is a need to expand the rehabilitative process to include social, emotional, intellectual, and vocational development. Future programs utilizing horticulture will aid the disabled and disadvantaged to adjust to the limitations of their disability, encourage them to develop an interest in their surroundings, and to find challenge and meaning in life through renewed confidence and achievement.

The Arboretum's program in "Therapy and Rehabilitation through Horticulture" consisted of two phases. The initial phase provided student-volunteers with a basic understanding of horticulture and its role in the rehabilitative process. Phase I of their training was conducted at UCONN'S Bartlett Arboretum. The second half of this training took place at the ESRCSC. Various faculty members, rehabilitative staff, physicians, therapists, community leaders, psychologists, and social workers were involved in the training program. Lectures and workshops included such topics as psychological aspects of horticultural therapy, use of horticulture as a therapeutic aid, elementary botany, basic materials and equipment for plant growth, analysis of basic planting routines, plant propagation, growing vegetables and flowers, insect and disease control, plant nutrition, forcing bulbs, planting terrariums, and use of plant material in arrangements. Phase II involved the implementation of horticultural knowledge and expertise gained under Phase I. These horticultural activities were designed to reinforce physical success made in other therapeutic areas in conjunction with social, psychological, and intellectual benefits. The student-volunteers interned at the ESRCSC, the Liberation House for drug abusers, the Franklin F. Dubois Day Treatment Center for the emotionally disturbed, Quintard Center for Senior Citizens, and the Norton School for children with learning disabilities.

The experience gained from this pilot program demonstrated quite conclusively that horticulture is a valuable medium which can be used therapeutically for both behavioral change and physical restoration in children, adults, and senior citizens. Hopefully, this program and others like it will serve as a model for future programs.

This book is designed to be a guide with suggestions and procedures for initiating and conducting a horticultural program for the disabled and disadvantaged. There is a section that describes the physical and psychological characteristics of various groups and their implications for horticulture, and an activity section that lists, codes and describes various horticultural activities and projects that can be adapted to meet the needs and capabilities of these various groups. The book will be of special aid to those studying in the fields of public recreation, occupational therapy, recreational therapy, social work, and special education. More specifically, it is intended to provide practical information that can be used by students in horticultural therapy, by volunteers and garden clubs who wish to begin a program, and by other community organizations and agencies that provide special services to the disabled and disadvantaged.

This book will achieve its purpose if it stimulates a better understanding of the needs of these groups, and if it motivates others to establish similar horticultural programs.

CONTENTS

HORTICULTURE
FOR THE DISABLED
AND DISADVANTAGED

Chapter One

PHILOSOPHY OF
HORTICULTURAL THERAPY

THE ROLE OF HORTICULTURE IN TODAY'S SOCIETY

THE great American horticulturist Liberty Hyde Bailey has characterized the field of horticulture as having three major aspects: the scientific or biological, the public or business, and the ornamental or aesthetic. Through the years, the emphasis has changed from one aspect to another. The scientific aspect has received the most attention. Horticulture is developing technology nourished by many sciences, and new, significant contributions have been made. The "Green Revolution" has resulted in high protein grains, improved hybrid varieties, and increased agricultural production. The business or public affairs aspect involves economics, and it is closely identified with higher standards of living and meeting the basic needs of society. Never before has there been more interest in growing vegetables, flowers, and houseplants. Experts in the field call this growing interest in home gardening a "horticultural revolution" that will alter the face of our nation and the lifestyle of our people. Indeed, many are calling this urge to return to the land, a "horticultural renaissance." The impetus for such a "revolution" is undoubtedly due to inflation, recession, and the energy crisis. Horticulture has also become a national craze with our young people. The "green scene" is certainly due to the concern for the environment and ecology and the vogue for organic foods. A more important factor is the rejection of materialistic values and the search for simpler and more rewarding interests. These attitudes are reflected in the aesthetic and human appeal of horticulture. Even though horticulture and its social implications have received the least attention, the values to this aspect of horticulture are likely to influence modern society in the future. These values deal with affection, with pleasure, with beauty, and with satisfaction. It is because of some of these values and their association with healing that medicine has turned to horticulture. Horticulture can be excellent therapy following an illness. The nervous tensions of modern living are reduced by creative and muscular outlets associated with gardening. Gardening can add beauty and serenity to the landscape of the human spirit by helping those in need find a more satisfying life.

Horticulture is a field that affects and influences all people in many ways. As society changes, there are pressures to find new ways to adjust and to meet the needs of everyday living. New skills and attitudes towards plants and gardening are emerging. It is imperative that the base of horticulture be broadened to include more than business, science, and art. Today's horticulture encompasses much more than "garden cultivation"; it can also contribute to the total life experience. Horticulture may become a vocation, a hobby, or a means for exercise and health. How we use plants in our everyday lives, in industry, and in solving many of today's problems will reflect this new role for horticulture.

> "Sow a seed, plant a bulb, raise a flower, grow a tree, harvest a crop of beauty. Isn't that a good way to help the world grow better?"
> — Ortho Chevron

HORTICULTURE — THERAPY — REHABILITATION

In the past, arts and crafts, music, and other recreational activities have been used for therapy. Horticulture used as therapy is probably the oldest of the activity therapies, but the last to be recognized for its merits. Today, the value of horticultural activities as another vehicle for therapy and rehabilitation is rapidly gaining recognition. The word "horto-therapy" was first used by Richardson Wright in 1945. It was first called "horticultural therapy" in 1948 by Ruth Mosher. Various other names have been used to distinguish this field of endeavor. Such titles as "flora therapy," "hort-therapy," "hortitherapy," and "horticultural therapy" are currently being employed.

Unfortunately, there is a great deal of confusion about what is therapy and what is therapeutic. Narrowly conceived, therapy is a medication, a surgery, or a treatment for a disease or behavioral difficulty. The present day concept of therapy includes total personality needs. It is concerned first with the individual and second with the disability itself. The universal aim is to help people by improving their physical and mental well-being. A situation may be therapeutic if it is structured to insure a predicted outcome. It may be direct or indirect, but the most beneficial results often occur indirectly. The term "rehabilitation" did not exist prior to World War I. It was previously referred to as "physical medicine." Like therapy, the present day concept emphasizes total rehabilitation. The objectives of rehabilitation are to improve the physical, mental, social, and vocational aptitudes so that a person can live happily and productively. Rehabilitation no longer has a beginning or an ending point. It has come to include many more services than it once did. Character development is just as important as the attainment of manual skills. Total rehabilitation means to live and to function again.

The basic problem in both therapy and rehabilitation is a psychiatric-mental health problem. The person engaged in horticultural therapy must realize that his patients or clients have trouble enjoying life without his help. Learning about the joy of living is essential to *all* people regardless of their disability. Dr. Karl Menninger sums it up best when he writes about the activity of therapists as "people who teach the art of living to persons who may never have quite learned it, or if so, have lost it for a time." The point here is that too much emphasis on what is therapy and what is therapeutic may destroy the spontaneous joy in helping others that is so important. If a person tries to be a therapist and deals in what he thinks as difficult, esoteric, and intellectual, this person is bound to communicate this feeling to his patients or clients. Then, the experience can hardly be considered therapeutic. Doing things we do best and with full enjoyment is the best way to make use of ourselves as therapeutic agents. The main challenge is to motivate any group of people in any setting and then use these responses to foster, maintain, and promote physical, social, and emotional health.

Horticulture used as therapy can be planned to provide specific therapeutic aims. It can be used for occupational therapy, for physical therapy, for recreational therapy, and for vocational therapy. The activities can be designed to meet the patient's needs; they can range from providing finger and manipulative activities to strenuous digging for those learning to use an artificial limb. Such activities are valuable because they tend to divert attention from the appliance to the activity. Moreover, it is possible to assess a patient's ability to walk, bend, lift, carry, and kneel, in addition to manual dexterity. The ability to comprehend instructions and to concentrate can also be assessed by observing the behavior and achievement in such activities. With careful planning, horticultural activities can become a useful aspect of the over-all therapeutic program.

PEOPLE AND PLANTS

The use of horticulture as an activity for therapy and rehabilitation is unique because the medium is living. Recent evidence indicates that there is an interplay between human behavior and garden activities. Plants, flowers, and trees satisfy some psychological need in man. Everyone is in daily contact with some form of plant life. Doctor Hugh Iltis, a taxonomist at the University of Wisconsin, believes that man is "genetically programmed" to require living plants in his surroundings. According to Doctor Iltis, "man, the animal, evolved in nature among plants, shrubs, trees, flowers and fruits, in a seasonal climate in which the living ecosystem was an integral part of his most basic being and functioning. Thus, civilized man needs these facets of the environment, not as luxuries and amenities, but as absolute and inalienable rights of his biological body." Other research in human behavior seems to indicate the existence of a symbiotic relationship between man and plants. Plants need man's care to develop best, but man also requires contact with plants to develop and maintain a mental wholeness. Plant life is a link that binds man to his world and to his environment.

The psychology of using plants for therapy and rehabilitation stems from the basic fact that growing living things fulfills certain needs in man. With respect to therapeutic and rehabilitative qualities of plants, Andrew Barber of the Menninger Foundation says, "germination of seeds, vegetative growth, flowering and maturation have close parallels to the basic concepts of human development. Common gardening tasks such as watering, fertilizing and protecting plants from bad weather also have human connotations. The physical structure of a greenhouse has been likened to a mother's womb and provides an atmosphere of security." Most humans react to plants in various ways. For some, growing and caring for plants presents a challenge. For the disabled and disadvantaged, plants provide living reality. It involves the acceptance of responsibility and a hope for achievement and success. Working with plants provides for experience in dealing with loss, which is a common therapeutic concern. Working with plants teaches patience; this delayed gratification is reflected in the slow but continuous and stable process of a plant producing a flower of beauty. Indeed, the discovery that new life can spring from a "dead" seed can stimulate determination and motivation to alter one's lifestyle. There is a quiet mystery to plant growth that helps one to relax and become more receptive to rehabilitation. In "Some Psychological Benefits of Gardening," Dr. Rachel Kaplan states that "activities such as growing seeds, rooting cuttings and potting plants require intense concentration of a type that produces a rest from the effort otherwise required for attention, and also provides rest from worries and cares in a person's mind."

With plants as a medium, social interaction is increased because it lends itself to group activity. It may be a small group in a hospital setting or it may be the disadvantaged in a ghetto planting a community garden. Whatever the setting, the activity provides for new experiences in living for many who have been deprived of human growth. Unfortunately, our society has been alienated from much of the living world. To the urban dweller and the disadvantaged, the growing of plants communicates deeper values in living in an environment that has been hostile to such values. Sociologists have defined some of the deficiencies of distressed urban areas. These include the need for stimulation to break the monotony of daily life, a need for a sense of community, and a need for mastery of one's surroundings so that one can have some control over what happens around him. It has been observed that many problems in urban areas can be alleviated by providing opportunities for people-plant interactions. As adviser to the New York City Housing Authority Tenant Garden Contest, Charles A. Lewis found that garden plots and related activities resulted in new attitudes toward the community. Vandalism was reduced in areas where there were gardens, and tenants took pride in their accomplishments by improving their buildings and grounds. In "Plants as Therapy," Elvin McDonald quotes Robert Steffen, farm manager for Father Flanagan's Boy's Home in Boy's Town, Nebraska:

> Gardening is good therapy for young and old. The earth has great healing power. It is the plant of course which makes it all possible. Simply realizing that we could not exist on this planet without the plant is significant. Learning how and why this is true can occupy much of a lifetime and be only a beginning. Plants are miraculous creations. They hold so many secrets that they present a challenge and a hope for men of all ages, rich and poor, learned and not so learned. Plants are indeed a source of great hope for our time and for the many people who are disturbed, frustrated and concerned about the future. Knowing and understanding plants can give them hope and reassurance that with death there follows life and the great cycles of seasons are part of even greater rhythms of the universe that are not dependent on mortal man's manipulation.

Overall, personal attitudes undergo a change as a result of working with plants. Individuals that can benefit the most are those under stress, either physical, psychological, or sociological. Their association with plants helps to alleviate their stress and create an atmosphere for health and improvement.

Chapter Two

PRINCIPLES OF
HORTICULTURAL THERAPY

HISTORY AND DEVELOPMENT OF
HORTICULTURAL THERAPY

MAN'S early interest in plants was based on their healing properties, and many of our earliest botanists and horticulturists were physicians who grew plants for their medicinal value.

The use of garden activities as preventive medicine has been in practice for many centuries. Before the science of psychiatry, physicians prescribed work in the garden for ills of the mind and nervous system. In 1798, Benjamin Rush believed that digging in the soil had a curative effect on the mentally ill. Hospitals in Spain, as early as 1806, observed that agricultural activities were beneficial to mental patients. At the turn of the century, programs were developed in many hospitals and institutions to make use of their grounds and farms, often resulting in therapeutic benefits. After World War I and II, veteran's hospitals used garden therapy for treatment and rehabilitation of disabled soldiers.

During the 1950s, the National Federation of Garden Clubs participated in volunteer programs using garden therapy in hospitals throughout the country. At this time, Michigan State University developed a master's degree program in horticultural therapy for occupational therapists. During the late 1950s, Miss Rhea McCandliss directed a full-time horticultural therapy program at the Menninger Clinic, and her efforts and interest were responsible for the formation of a national horticultural therapy organization.

In 1971, the first undergraduate program in horticultural therapy in the United States was offered at Kansas State University in cooperation with the Menninger Foundation.

In 1973, The National Council for Therapy and Rehabilitation through Horticulture was organized to promote and encourage the development of horticulture and related activities as a therapeutic and rehabilitative medium. The National Council's membership consists of more than 400 organizations and individuals, including the Menninger Clinic, New York University's Institute for Rehabilitation Medicine, and the horticultural departments of many universities. The Council's headquarters is located in Mount Vernon, Virginia.

The demand for trained horticultural therapists has influenced horticultural departments of major universities to offer both undergraduate and graduate degrees in horticultural therapy. They include the universities of Florida, Maryland, Tennessee, Kansas State, Texas, and Clemson University. Accreditation and/or certification of students in horticultural therapy is needed to further improve the image and status of this new profession.

Many training schools have programs in horticulture. The Melwood Horticultural Training Center in Upper Marlboro, Maryland teaches horticultural skills to mentally retarded, young adults, and has been praised by HEW for developing basic work skills and job responsibility with these individuals. The Veteran's Administration, which maintains the largest hospital network in the world, utilizes horticulture as a therapeutic medium in approximately 21 percent of their hospitals. Horticultural therapy is also being carried on in public schools in special education classes and in ecology workshops.

Programs in horticultural therapy offer the opportunity to improve the quality of life in urban, suburban, and even in rural areas. Inner city projects, gardens for the blind, and other community projects such as the Washington Youth Gardens have experienced such benefits.

Today, numerous schools, hospitals, arboreta, community centers, and correctional institutions are using horticulture for educational, therapeutic, and recreational purposes. In the future, innovative programs, research in man-plant interactions, biofeedback, and other areas of psychological and physical effects of plants will be very important in the growth, development, and sophistication of horticultural therapy.

THE HORTICULTURAL THERAPIST

Characteristics

A horticultural therapist, according to Rhea McCandliss, is "one who uses the knowledge of plants and gardening, greenhouse and floristry skills as a tool to develop a relationship with a patient for the dual purpose of helping that patient with the problem of adjustment, and encouraging the patient to develop a broader interest in his surroundings as a result of increased knowledge of the plant world." A horticultural therapist does not have to possess a special kind of understanding or personality. The major goal is to develop effective human relationships. This requires empathy, fairness, humor, honesty, humility, intelligence, self-confidence, and tact. The effective therapist is cheerful, well adjusted, and respectful of other opinions.

The Menninger Foundation and Kansas State University have formulated some basic characteristics of a good horticultural therapist:

1. "A person who likes to work with people." This means all kinds of people that may differ in age, sex, race, disability, cultural and economic backgrounds. It may involve working with one individual or with groups. Your role may vary from an active leader to that of a consultant.

2. "A person who has compassion and patience in helping others." It often means the patients helping themselves. Sometimes a patient will not respond, and the therapist must be patient and persistent in order to procure proper responses.

3. "A person who has knowledge of the skills and practices of modern horticulture and the ability to transmit this knowledge to others." It is wise to avoid formal lecture techniques. Demonstrations seem to be the most effective. Give directions in the form of requests, not demands. Be sure to include suggestions that will increase the chances for success. Often it is neces-

sary to use indirect as well as direct methods to gain participation; for example, ask someone to assist. Do not try to teach and motivate a patient or student by saying, "It's good for you." Include activities requiring simple responses which need few directions and involve simple repetition of movements.

4. "A person who is resourceful in developing new approaches and innovative projects to involve people in horticultural interests." This includes activities with reasonable goals which allow for satisfaction, achievement, and prestige. It involves the ability to motivate. The activities should be planned to meet the needs of an individual rather than for cases or diseases. Provide activities that encourage all levels of participation — active, passive, and spectator, both indoors and outdoors. Plan activities around an area that the individual can relate to, such as a ghetto-community garden, a hospital flower garden, or a bedside terrarium.

5. "A person who knows himself and has confidence in what he can do." A therapist must not confuse his own needs with those he observes in his patients or clients. An appearance of anxiety and apprehension in the therapist often upsets the patients.

6. "A person who keeps a professional, warm, but objective attitude toward another's problems." One must have indulgence and must often excuse a patient's actions, but at the same time also have a casual recognition of a patient's conduct. This requires basic understanding, not pity. Be aware of a patient's susceptibility to emotional involvement, and avoid relationships of too personal a nature.

7. "A person who can work closely with other staff members toward a common goal." The horticultural program should be thought of as one aspect of the total therapeutic and rehabilitative process. There should be an emphasis on reinforcing gains made in other therapeutic areas whether they be physical, intellectual, social, or psychological. The therapist must learn to observe behavior so that, at review or "rap-up" sessions, he is able to report objectively concerning the reactions of his students, clients, or patients, and the situations in which the reactions occurred.

Training and Experience

Many believe that there is a need to establish a set of standards involving specific educational requirements and clinical experience in order to be qualified as a horticultural therapist. Basically, this need for accreditation and certification stems from the desire to improve the image and status of this new profession. Some universities have already developed curricula that train a student in the areas of horticulture and psychology, in addition to practical internship. The main objective is to prepare these students so that they can obtain potential employment in an institution that desires the aid of a horticultural therapist. However, the requirements set down by an institution may vary just as much as the definitions differ for the person known as a "horticultural therapist." Most agree that formal training in horticulture with practical experience in therapy is desirable. A degree in horticulture with a minor in occupational therapy, plus practical experience, is one answer. However, a degree in occupational therapy with a minor in horticulture is just as valid. At this point in time, a person who desires a professional title should research the various institutions, listed in Table I, that offer degree programs. For those persons who already have a related background and/or have an avid interest in working with people through the medium of horticulture as a volunteer, an activity leader, or as a therapeutic aide, the following criteria are suggested:

1. A basic understanding of the nature, significance, and values of a program in horticultural therapy.

2. A familiarity with other related programs.

3. A knowledge of techniques and methods used in organizing and conducting a program in horticultural therapy. Attending workshops can be very beneficial.

4. An in-service training program is essential. This may involve weekly sessions including lectures, demonstrations, and discussions to share new ideas and techniques.

In the future, it is mandatory that the National Council set down standards for certification so that graduates are well qualified to work as "horticulturists," horticultural therapists,"

Table I: Universities in the United States which have
degree programs in horticultural therapy.

University	Location
Clemson University	Clemson, South Carolina
Michigan State University	Lansing, Michigan
Kansas State University	Manhattan, Kansas
University of Maryland	College Park, Maryland

"social horticulturists," "therapeutic horticulturists," "therapists," or whatever the case may be!

The Use of Vounteers

Experience has shown that horticultural programs in some institutions can be conducted with a minimum of professional staff and with a great deal of assistance from volunteers. Many volunteers are truly dedicated and possess unique skills that can enrich and expand the services available to patients and clients. They represent new faces and often have refreshing approaches to activities. They often have additional interests in the community that may benefit the program concerning operation and implementation. Volunteers that are members of garden clubs have proven to be effective horticultural therapists. For many years, garden clubs have sponsored horticultural therapy programs in hospitals, nursing homes, schools for the physically and mentally handicapped, and at many other facilities where their talents are needed. They have also sponsored workshops and seminars on horticultural therapy. Regardless of why they volunteer, their life is made fuller by seeing examples of their fellow man reaching out for a more productive life. Because of this, many volunteers have decided to spend their professional future in the field of therapy and rehabilitation.

"Give fools their gold and knaves their power,

Let fortune's bubbles rise and fall;
Who sows a field or trains a flower,
or plants a tree is more than all."

— Whittier

PROGRAM DEVELOPMENT

Organization and Operation

There are certain preliminary steps that must be taken before an individual or group begins to organize a program in horticultural therapy.

DETERMINE THE NEED AND PROCURE A SPONSOR. You must know the facts about the disabled and disadvantaged and the services that are available to them in the community. Consult various institutions, hospitals, and community centers. Conduct a survey of existing programs in the community with the aid of garden clubs and other service groups. Get as many agencies and groups involved and interested as possible.

ADVERTISE THE PROGRAM. Send representatives to various institutions to discuss a proposed program. This meeting should include the nature and scope of the program, its desired outcome, who will conduct it, and finances. Use public relations media such as the newspaper, newsletters, television, and radio to advertise the program.

FINANCING THE PROGRAM. Consider foundations, auxiliaries, and other service clubs for necessary finances. The program may be self-sufficient by selling various items that are created and grown in the program. Consult local businessmen for donations, discounts, and possible outlets for sales. A free guide for those interested in raising funds on a local level is "Local Fund Development: A Basic Manual for Volunteer Programs," available from the National Center for Voluntary Action, 1785 Massachusetts Avenue, N.W., Washington, D.C. 20036. Also, a list of foundations for possible funding is available from The National Foundation Center, New York, N.Y. 10017.

Program Planning

1. Plan a program of activities that meets the needs of a particular group. Consider age (children, adolescents, senior citizens), sex, and cultural background. Consider the disability, but plan and improvise a program so that this is only a secondary concern.

2. Provide activities and projects that are both active and passive for both indoors and outdoors.

3. Limit the size of the group and consider the ratio of leaders to participants (1:1, 1:2, etc.)

4. Determine a schedule (once a week) and a time-limit (30 minutes to an hour) for the sessions. Avoid haste. Be alert for fatigue and boredom. Allow time for cleanup.

5. Be aware of the need for long-range planning and preparation for certain activities and projects.

6. Make use of all available community resources such as the library, films, slides, botanical gardens and arboreta, museums, and garden experts.

7. Have the participants contribute to the planning of the activities. Experience has shown that a club with its own name is important to the patients and clients.

8. Consider the possibility of having a chairperson for the month who is responsible for planning the month's activities with others assisting.

9. Keep your sponsors informed of the program's progress.

10. Always evaluate and revise the program.

GOALS AND OBJECTIVES

The specific goals and objectives of a program in horticultural therapy may differ distinctly from one institution to another and from one group of disabled and disadvantaged individuals to another. Diane Hefley, president of the National Council for Therapy and Rehabilitation through Horticulture, has listed the objectives and benefits that a program should stress. These benefits are intellectual, social, emotional, and physical development.

Intellectual Benefits

1. "Attainment of new skills." The field of horticulture offers the opportunity to learn various methods and techniques that may lead to a new hobby or to a vocation.

2. "Improved vocabulary and communication skills." Experiencing new activities and projects results in learning new terms and concepts. The classification and naming of plants can help improve these skills.

3. "Aroused sense of curiosity." Plants provide a medium for experimentation.

4. "Increased powers of observation." This involves a new awareness of the environment and basic relationships between living things. The ability to notice small differences is enhanced by working with plants. The arrangement of plants in a pot can be used to diagnose spatial ability and number concept, in addition to memory and concentration.

5. "Vocational and prevocational training." Learning new horticultural skills may lead to a new vocation in the community.

6. "Stimulation of sensory perception." All the senses are aroused in a horticultural therapy program, resulting in an increased sensitivity to the immediate environment. Those with perceptual problems can improve their ability to look and observe.

Social Benefits

1. "Interaction within the group." Working toward a common goal provides for increased group interaction. Group members learn responsibility, cooperation, and respect for the rights of others.

2. "Interactions outside of the group." Field trips provide an opportunity to interact with others, and sharing their accomplishments provides for self-esteem. A horticultural interest can enable a person to take part in community activities again.

Emotional Growth

1. "Improved confidence and self-esteem." All activities can be planned so that there is a great degree of success and achievement.

2. "Opportunities to relieve aggressive drives in a socially acceptable manner." Working in the garden can relieve tension, frustrations, and aggression.

3. "Activities which promote interest and enthusiasm for the future." Specific activities provide for an atmosphere of anticipation and a new interest in tomorrow. People can be useful to plants, and, in turn, help to beautify the environment.

4. "Opportunities for the satisfaction of creative drives." Many latent or hidden talents for self-expression and creativity are revealed in flower arranging, bonsai, and other activities. There is also great satisfaction by being able to contribute something to someone or to society.

Physical Benefits

1. "Development and improvement of basic motor skills." Horticultural activities can be planned to provide specific therapeutic benefits.

2. "Increased outdoor activities." Activities outdoors can improve physical and mental health.

FACILITIES, EQUIPMENT AND SUPPLIES

Special facilities and elaborate equipment are not necessary for a program in horticultural therapy. Slight modifications are, however, very beneficial. The key to success is to improvise whenever possible.

Facilities

Use *paths* and *ramps* instead of steps. The gradient of the paths should not exceed 5 percent, and they should be at least three feet wide and constructed of a nonslip material such as brushed concrete, asphalt, or patio bricks.

Raised beds greatly increase the capability of the wheelchair gardener and those that cannot bend. The height of the beds can be adjusted to suit the individual's need. Raised beds should be at least two feet high, but not wider than four feet if worked on both sides, and not wider than two feet if they are against a wall. The beds can be made of bricks, slabs of concrete, paving stones, or railroad ties. Rectangular raised beds are the easiest to construct. Barrels and tubs of appropriate height can also be used. Refer to the Activity Section — Gardening in Raised Beds and Containers — for additional information and suggestions.

Gardening in a *greenhouse* is particularly suitable for the disabled because of the controlled climate. If a greenhouse is available, it should be designed to meet the needs of the disabled. The path down the center should be at least two and one-half feet wide, and the benches should be two feet wide and two feet high. It is suggested that a "herringbone" pattern for the benches be used to maximize growing space. The door should be two and one-half feet wide, and sliding doors have been found to be more convenient than hinged doors. There should be no obstructions at the ground level. A wide turning area should be outside the greenhouse so that a wheelchair can easily be turned around. The following wheelchair specifications may be helpful in planning such a facility:

Typical adult wheelchair specifications:
    Length: 42 inches
    Width: 26 inches
    Height of seat: 19.5 inches
    Height of armrest: 29 inches
    Height of rear pusher handles: 36 inches
Functioning measurements of a wheelchair:
    Fixed turning radius: 18 inches (wheel to wheel)
    Fixed turning radius: 31.5 inches (front structure to rear)
    Average turning space: 60 inches x 60 inches
    60 inches minimum width for two wheelchairs to pass each other.

Adult individual functioning in a wheelchair:
Unilateral vertical reach: average 60 inches
Horizontal working reach: average 30.8 inches
Bilateral horizontal reach: average 64.5 inches
Diagonal reach on the wall: average 48 inches from the floor

Use small plastic garbage cans or standard galvanized cans for storage of media in the greenhouse. These containers can be angled or hinged under the benches.

A study of barrier-free site design by the American Society of Landscape Architects for the Department of Housing and Urban Development has resulted in a text by Jay Jorgensen entitled, "Landscape Design for the Disabled." A set of slides, tape-cassette, and a guidebook are also available which deal with "Landscape Design to Accommodate the Handicapped," also by Jay Jorgensen. These can be obtained from: The Publication Department, ASLA Foundation, 1750 Old Meadow Road, McLean, Virginia 22101.

Provide *resting benches* near a garden or meditation area.

Equipment

Use light-weight equipment and supplies for those with physical limitations. Heavier equipment can be used for those that need to strengthen a weak arm or hand, and to improve their work-tolerance.

Short-handled tools are helpful for children and for those in wheelchairs working on a raised garden. The handles should have rubber grips that are extra thick for those with weak grips. A kneeler or support is very helpful to work in a conventional garden. Light-weight, long-handled tools are preferred for those that must work from a wheelchair. Tools with telescopic handles and with adjustable handle-lengths are available from Wolf Tool Ltd., Ross on Wye, Herefordshire, England. Extra handle grips on shovels and other tools help to improve coordination when working. Rachet-action tools can be ordered from: Rachet-cut, P.O. Box 303, Milldale, Connecticut 06467.

A movable push cart with storage areas for tools, media, and other supplies is very useful. A two-wheel cart can be constructed with handles that attach to the armrest of the wheelchair so that heavy objects can be transported while using both hands to push the wheelchair.

A removable work satchel can be attached to the back of a wheelchair for transporting light-weight equipment tools and supplies.

Wheelbarrows should be two wheeled, lightweight, and have either a pram handle or a single handle for this type can be used by those who have the use of only one hand.

In general, very simple modifications of common articles and appliances are sufficient to allow the disabled to take part in gardening activities. For example, a piece of hollow metal tubing can be used to plant seeds by those who cannot bend; the seeds are directed to fall down through the tube to the desired location on the surface of the soil. The ability to improvise and to make use of various materials is the key to success.

Plant Materials

To select the proper plant material, consider the following: (1) The availability of light. (2) The availability of space. Use miniature plants and varieties if space is limited. (3) Plants should be colorful, fast growing, flowering and easy to care for.

It is best to use common names for plants, particularly with individuals with speech problems.

Refer to the Activity Section for suggested plants for a particular activity. Consult the Resource Section for suppliers of seeds, bulbs, and plants.

Supplies

The following is a list of supplies that are commonly needed in a horticultural therapy program.

Bags (burlap, paper, plastic)
Baskets (fruit)
Blotters
Books (telephone)

Bone meal or superphosphate
Borax
Bottle caps (for mini-arrangements)
Bottle cutter
Bottles (wine, Windex® — for sprayer)
Brushes
Buckets (plastic or metal)
Bulb glasses and bulb pans
Burlap

Cement (Duco®, mason)
Chalk
Charcoal
Cheesecloth
Chicken wire
Cigar boxes
Clay (molding)
Clips (paper)
Clothespins
Coat hangers (for terrarium tools)
Contac® paper (clear)
Containers (milk, margarine, yogurt, tin)
Cord
Cornmeal
Cotton
Crockery and chards
Cups (plastic and Styrofoam®)

Dishes (bonsai)
Drills
Dyes

Egg cartons

Felt
Fertilizer (5-10-5, 20-20-20)
Flats (wooden or plastic)
Floral picks
Forks

Glass panes
Glasses (plastic)

Gloves
Glue (Elmer's®)
Gravel

Hammer
Hardware cloth (wire mesh)
Hoes
Hormones (Rootone® Hormodine® 1,2,3)
Hose (garden)

Jars
Jugs (gallon — glass or plastic)

Knives

Label maker and tapes
Labels (plastic and wooden)
Lights (fluorescent)
Loppers

Magnifying glass
Marble chips
Market packs (5.5 x 7.75 in.)
Mirrors (pocket)
Misters

Oasis
Oil cloth
Orris root powder

Paint
Paper (cardboard, construction, drawing, newspaper, tissue)
Peat moss and sheet moss
Peat pellets (Jiffy 7®, Jiffy 9®, Solo-Gro® cubes, Kys-Kube®)
Pencils (drawing, waterproof)
Perlite
PH kit
Picks (floral)
Picture frames
Pie pans (aluminum)
Pins (fern)
Pipe cleaners

Plaster of paris
Plastic flowers
Plastic sheets or covers
Pots (clay, plastic, Styrofoam, peat)

Rakes
Razor blades
Ribbon
Rubber bands
Rulers

Salt
Sand (mason, Terrasand®)
Scissors
Seed tapes
Shears
Shellac
Shovels
Silica gel
Soil
Spices
Sponges
Spoons (plastic, metal)
Spray (acrylic, artificial snow)
Sprayer
Sprinkler
Stakes (bamboo, plastic, and wooden)
Stapler and staples
Styrofoam

Tacks (thumb)
Tags
Tape (clear, masking, floral, corsage)
Terrarium tools (astrofingers, forceps)
Test tubes and floral tubes
Timer (plant)
Toothbrushes
Toothpicks
Towels (paper)
Trays (Styrofoam, plastic)

Trowels
Twine (garden and macrame)
Twistems®

Vermiculite

Watering can
Wax (grafting)
Window boxes
Wire (floral)
Wire baskets
Wire cutter
Wood (plywood, lattice)

A PROGRAM SCHEDULE

A program in horticultural therapy can be planned on a monthly basis with appropriate activities for each month. The following schedule for one year is an example.

January
1. Introduce gardening under lights
2. Make bird feeders
3. Make flower arrangements
4. Show colored slides or a film
5. Distribute garden catalogs

February
1. Sow seeds of coleus, geraniums, cacti, and African violets (grow these under artificial lights).
2. Make gifts for Valentine's Day
3. Make dish gardens and miniature landscapes
4. Bring in flowering branches to be forced

March
1. Start cuttings and air layer
2. Bring in potted bulbs
3. Sow vegetable, flower, and herb seeds
4. Do sand paintings

April
1. Introduce hydroponics
2. Plan the garden plot

3. Prepare the garden plot
4. Transplant seedlings

May

1. Make gifts for Mother's Day
2. Trim shrubs on the grounds
3. Plant flower and vegetable gardens
4. Have a May Market
5. Graft cacti

June

1. Plant hanging baskets
2. Take a field trip to a park or arboretum
3. Maintain and cultivate the gardens
4. Plant window boxes

July

1. Have a picnic
2. Make planters
3. Begin to harvest vegetables
4. Start a topiary
5. Introduce pest control

August

1. Start to gather dried plant materials
2. Plant seed of biennials and perennials
3. Pick and dry flowers for future arrangements
4. Make potpourri

September

1. Make ecology boxes
2. Have a harvest picnic
3. Introduce bonsai
4. Take cuttings of border plants for house plants

October

1. Make a terrarium
2. Make dried arrangements and plaques
3. Plant bulbs for forcing
4. Process gourds and carve pumpkins
5. Make a compost pile

November

1. Pot up paperwhites for a December bloom
2. Make Thanksgiving decorations

3. Have a plant clinic
4. Do some "kitchen gardening"
December
1. Gather materials for Christmas decorations
2. Make Christmas gifts and cards
3. Arrange winter greens
4. Have a Christmas party

A CHILDREN'S PROGRAM

At the present time, there are over seven million disabled children in the United States, not including the gifted and those who are disadvantaged by societal or economic conditions. Their handicaps may be emotional, mental, physical, or social, and each particular handicap interferes with a child's ability to learn. In law and as national policy, children have a right to education that is designed for their particular needs and aspirations.

A child experiences half of his learning before four years of age, another 30 percent before eight, and only 20 percent during the remaining years of elementary and secondary education. The normal development of *all* children is implemented by providing activities that are both interesting and educational. Children must be exposed to various experiences and be encouraged to participate in many activities. Horticultural activities combine manual manipulation with mental challenge in addition to exploratory experiences. Various programs in horticulture can teach children how to get along with people, how to respect the rights of others, and how to assume responsibility.

Dereck Fell, director of the National Garden Bureau, states that "gardening gives children a creative outlet that keeps them out of mischief and teaches them self-help." Children are naturally creative, but they need guidance to realize their maximum potential development. Horticultural activities offer creative outdoor recreation in many forms: discovery of the wonder of growing living things, a closeness to nature, and projects that result in pride by creating beauty. This proves to be therapy for

both the well and the disabled. Through gardening, a troubled
child learns to relate to the world outside of his own injured
personality. Children experience a new level of participation in
life that makes them sense their own importance and accomplishment because they realize that growing plants are dependent upon them. Inner-city youths experience a new
self-image by knowing that they have contributed something
constructive to society by improving the environment through
gardening. Such a medium of instruction which develops re-
sourcefulness in a child is worthy of consideration.

Some children take to gardening more than others, but most
children at one age or another are interested in digging in the
soil and planting a seed. Children inherently have a desire to
work with living things. It is unfortunate that many city
children have never planted a seed or watched a plant grow.
Children in the cities need gardening activities as part of their
education for life. Thinking citizens of many communities are
seeking ways to provide their children with experiences which
will lead to useful living. Every activity in the garden provides
opportunities for the development of responsibility and an appreciation for work. Children seek activities that are rich in
work as well as in fun. In a garden setting, a child becomes
physically involved, and he learns how to work. More important, the child learns directly; one does not learn about seeds,
but actually sows them. A child learns that plants have needs
just as a person has, and by observing how plants grow and
change, a child can better understand his own growth.

A garden program can be conducted by schools or by community and neighborhood youth gardening programs. An example is the Cleveland Garden Program which began in 1904.
It provides young people with individual garden plots for
growing flowers and vegetables. Last year, 21,000 Cleveland
school children participated and harvested over $600,000 worth
of vegetables that they grew themselves. Another is "Garden
Hilltop," a program that was started 25 years ago by Indiana
University, in cooperation with the city's Department of Parks
and Recreation and the Bloomington Garden Club. Here the

city's children and teachers learn together about the various aspects of indoor and outdoor gardening. Other successful programs are those at the Brooklyn Botanical Garden and the Washington Youth Gardens.

To start a program in your community, talk to leaders of various civic groups, community-related individuals, and garden club leaders for support. Approach the city, business firms, or other interested individuals for appropriate funds or for land.

Guidelines for a Successful Program

1. Let children experiment and learn from both success and failure. You will realize that from a child's point of view, there really are no failures in gardening because, whatever happens, it will be interesting.
2. It is easier to relate to children when you explore with them instead of dictating to them. To learn together and to set the atmosphere, begin the lesson with "Let's find out."
3. Discipline in a garden should seldom be a problem. You will find that the young gardener responds happily to simple, well-planned activities.
4. Remember that both plants and children grow in a garden. The emphasis can be on the garden or on the children, but equal emphasis usually brings the best results.

Refer to the Activity Section — Children's Gardening Activities and Community Gardening — for additional guidelines and suggestions.

"Children are people — They grow into tomorrow only as they live today."

— John Dewey

"People murder a child when they say, 'Keep out of the dirt.' In dirt there is life."

— George Washington Carver

A HORTICULTURAL PROGRAM FOR DISABLED
CHILDREN 4 TO 7: SCHOOL-READINESS GROUP*

The following is an example of an experimental internship program carried on by a trained volunteer in horticultural therapy.

Purpose of the Program:

To use horticulture as a therapy aid for physically disabled children of school-readiness age. The goals for this age group are modest, but the possibilities are enormous. A year-long program is planned with time regularly scheduled (two or three times a week) on a one-to-one basis with volunteer assistance. Attention will be given to seasonal activities. One-hour sessions are planned.

I. *Introduction*
Give children name tags in the shape of a maple or an oak leaf. Tell the children about the program. Talk about plants, flowers, trees, fruits, and vegetables. Cut and paste activity: use seed and nursery catalogs and construction paper, or draw with crayons. Be sure there is something for each child to take home and talk about with his family.

II. *Field Trip*
Take walks around the garden, greenhouse, arboretum — wherever the children are able to go. Collect leaves, flowers, cones, weeds, and grasses. Make a classroom display and some take-home projects with this material.

III. *Discussion*
What is a plant? Describe and show flower parts and leaves, stems, roots, seedpods and tubers. How does a plant eat? How does the sunlight play a part? This program will require a ready supply of natural material so that the children can handle the plants and flowers while the teacher talks.

IV. *Start plants for the classroom*
Here we will use our propagation and potting procedures.
1. Plant seeds. Select seeds that are large and easy to handle,

---

*A program conducted at the Easter Seal Rehabilitation Center of Southwestern Connecticut.

such as beans and nasturtiums.

2. Transplant small plants. The Kalanchoe variety that produces new plants at the tips and margins of its leaves is an ideal plant, and they are indestructible!

3. Cress farms in clean vermiculite are very successful. Sprouted citrus seeds grow well in soil. Bean sprouts are fast and easy too. Fairly fast results are necessary with children.

4. A single, large bean planted in vermiculite along the side of a clear plastic cup makes a great visual lesson when it sprouts.

5. Philodendrons, German and Swedish Ivy will root rapidly in a clear container of water.

6. Plan a comparison of seeds left in dark versus light, or plants given too much versus too little water.

V. *Plant care*

Periodic check of growing projects, including watering, feeding, cultivating, and checking for insects and disease. Since self-identity and possession are important to children, each child should have his own plant(s), spoon to work with, possibly his own apron (another volunteer project!), and watering can or sprayer to be shared. This phase of the program goes on throughout the school year.

VI. *Coordinated programs and projects*

Books, stories, and records about plants can be read and played during the rest period.

Scrapbooks can be made with leaves, dried flowers, drawing cut-outs, and paste-ups.

Show and Tell — bring in things from home and discuss these. Decorate and prepare containers to pot plants for Christmas, Valentine's Day, and Easter. Use flowering bulbs, paperwhite narcissus for springtime projects.

Indoor vegetable gardening: plant carrot and beet tops, hollowed-out sweet potatoes, avocado seeds, pineapple tops, radishes, beans, and cress seeds.

Caveats

The materials used in working with children must be carefully chosen. Familiar, everyday objects such as an old spoon for a trowel and colorful cups for pots are easy to obtain. Lots of newspaper, pasteurized soil, and a place to wash hands are necessary. Have small water containers to hold down spillage. Avoid known allergy irritants such as goldenrod, and all poisonous plants such as Jerusalem cherry.

AN EXPERIMENTAL HORT-THERAPY PROGRAM FOR A SHELTERED WORKSHOP GROUP*

The following program of activities was planned and directed by trained volunteers who called themselves "hortihelpers." There were three volunteer-leaders and 4 to 7 participants. Each session lasted from one to two hours.

Week I

Project: Sprouting mung beans

Materials: mung beans, small and large aluminum cake pans, cheese cloth, Baggies®, Twistems.

Procedure: Puncture bottom of the small aluminum pans. Set this pan in a larger pan which is pinched in at the sides to support the inner pan above the bottom. Place moist cheesecloth in the pan, and then sprinkle mung beans on top. Water is also placed in the bottom pan, and each unit is sealed in a plastic bag with a Twistem. The project is to be taken home and kept in the dark for a week.

Results: There was great interest. The concept of pinching in the sides of the pans was difficult for some. Some could not manage the Twistems.

Project: Sprouting lima beans in a glass

Materials: bean seeds, blotter, and glass containers.

Procedure: A blotter is slipped into a glass, and four beans are inserted between the blotter and the glass and then moistened. The project is to be taken home to observe how seeds sprout.

Results: Even spacing of the beans and not tearing the blotter were the major problems, but they managed.

---

*A program for physically and mentally disabled adults at the Easter Seal Rehabilitation Center of Southwestern Connecticut.

Project: Find a name for our group

Precedure: After becoming acquainted, we discussed a name. "Junior Arboretum" was too pretentious. "Green Thumbers" was selected as a name.

Project: Forcing magnolia branches for flowers

Procedure: Forcing was discussed, and the branches were trimmed, placed in water, and then put in a dark place.

Week II

Project: Make chop suey

Materials: chop suey recipe, knives, cutting boards, frying pans, plates, and forks.

Procedure: Discussed plant material used in the recipe which included green peppers, onions, scallions, celery, mushrooms, and beans. Each participant cut up one vegetable, and we passed it around during the talk. We sautéed the chicken, and then asked each participant to bring up his vegetable and put it in the pan. We ate the mixture on chinese noodles.

Results: Delicious! The idea of cooking has resulted in a separate activity group at the Center known as "cooking therapy."

Week III

Project: Peanut butter pine cones for birds

Materials: Pine cones, peanutbutter mixture (1 part peanut butter, 2 parts lard or cooking grease, 4 parts corn meal).

Procedure: Spread the peanutbutter mixture on the pine cones, and tie a string on the top.

Results: Although is was explained that the mixture was for the birds and tasted awful, they all ate a fingerful when we were not looking, and they all agreed that it did indeed taste awful!

Project: pine cone birds

Materials: pine cones, glue, pipe cleaners, feathers, paper.

Procedure: Use the pine cones for the bodies, the pipe cleaners for the legs, the feathers for the tails, and the paper to shape a beak.

Results: Needed assistance to a large extent.

Project: Dried flower arrangement

Materials: cans, Contact paper, sand, dried plant materials.

Procedure: Covered cans with Contac paper, filled with sand, and placed dried flowers and weeds of their choice in the cans.

Results: Very successful.

Week IV

Project: Planting bulbs of paper-white narcissus

Procedure: Place a bulb in the container with water and gravel up to its root crown. Place the bulbs in the dark until roots have filled the container.

Project: Forcing pussy willows

Procedure: Place branches in water and set aside for all to watch.

Follow-up: Checked magnolias; they had bloomed.

Week V

Project: Sowing seeds

Procedure: Prepare flats with soil and sow the seeds. Each person selected what he wanted from an assortment of vegetables and flowers. Mark the flats with the name of the gardener and plants. Place the flats in large plastic bags.

Project: Pole-bean teepee

Procedure: Four beans were planted in large pots, and a teepee was made of three garden stakes so that the plants could grow and climb them.

Results: They really enjoy the "dirt" projects. Fastening the top of the teepee sticks together presented a small problem.

Follow-up: Placed the narcissus bulbs in the light, and asked the group to check for water.

Week VI

Project: Sow radish seeds outdoors

Materials: Digging tools and seeds.

Procedure: Prepared a garden plot against the foundation wall of the Center. The bed was 6 feet by 18 inches.

Results: A marvelous project. Placed a stool for one individual so that he could work without standing. Also, placed papers to kneel on.

Project: Movie — "Wonders of Plant Growth"

Materials: Movie from public library, projector, and screen.

Follow-up: Checked pussy willows and narcissus bulbs. One individual of the group has taken on the responsibility of watering. We told her what a good job she is doing.

Week VII

Project: Flower arranging

Materials: 12 tulips, 3 bunches of white and 3 bunches of yellow chrysanthemums, 1 bunch of white daisies, 1 bunch of green ferns, clippers, plastic containers, oasis.

Procedure: One of us demonstrated each step of the arrangement. We had five participants, each with identical flowers, and it took two of us every minute to assist them.

Results: Some had difficulty understanding where to cut the stems and how to insert them into the oasis. The arrangements were excellent, and the participants were very proud of their results.

Week VIII

Project: Dish gardens and terrariums

Materials: Containers, perlite, soil, small plants, moss, rocks, shells, small figurines, mirrors, tools.

Procedure: Place adequate drainage material and soil in the container. The plants used were rooted cuttings which the participants had prepared earlier. Small figurines, stones and shells were used for accessory decorations. Miniature lakes were made with pocket mirrors surrounded with Plasticene®.

Results: One of the best sessions.

Follow-up: admired pussy willows and narcissus. Transplanted vegetables and flowers they had earlier grown from seed.

General Conclusions

Plan ahead to develop continuity, and the projects should be followed-up. Do not drop a project once the session is over. When we sprouted lima beans in a glass, we should have planned a session on planting them in pots, and perhaps another session on moving them outdoors and staking.

Bring a sample of the project so that the group can see what it will look like when it is completed. Encourage bringing plant materials from home to share with others. When projects do go home, make sure that you have extras if they forget to bring them back again. Also encourage your participants to take as much responsibility as possible in helping to set up, getting supplies, helping each other, and cleaning up. Once they understand what is needed, the group is usually happy to help.

Develop a kit of permanent supplies by observing what materials are used more than once.

SETTING UP A PROGRAM FOR THE
SEVERELY HANDICAPPED AND RETARDED*

The past six months at Shoreline have been an enlightening experience for me and for the young adults working to further develop the horticulture program at STEM (Shoreline Training and Employment).

When I first came to STEM in July, 1975, I spent some time familiarizing myself with the staff, the trainees, and the general method of operation. During this time, my first objective became clear to me. I wished to evaluate and to determine which trainees might best benefit from a horticultural therapy program. My initial group of trainees then became those who were not suited for the other employment-oriented programs at STEM. These included severely handicapped and retarded persons as well as trainees with severe emotional problems.

Considering the trainees I had selected, I was certainly faced with some challenging problems. I promptly recognized the benefits these individuals would derive from individual attention, and I therefore devised a buddy system of work-learning. This system employed volunteers working on a one-to-one or small group basis with the trainees. The volunteers I selected were themselves interested in horticulture and were thereby able to convey their enthusiasm to the trainees; higher level trainees, more proficient in various types of greenhouse management skills, assisted their coworkers. These symbiotic relationships proved beneficial to all, as individual learning problems were

---

*A program developed by Eleanor Pascalides, Horticultural Therapist, STEM Services, Gilford, Connecticut. "I" refers to Ms. Pascalides in the text.

dealt with in a personalized manner. An example of this is the case of one trainee previously employed in our training for the employment segment of STEM's horticulture program. Due to her difficulties in communicating verbally, it was felt that she would benefit more in a program where she would be required to verbally express herself. As a high level trainee working in the greenhouse, she was assigned skills such as weeding and potting plants. Motivated by her new responsibility, she has made notable strides in communicative skills. As in this individual's case, noticeable behavior changes have occurred in many of the trainees working under the buddy system.

Now that I felt I had arrived at a productive work-learning system, I needed to consider my next objective. This was the design of a structured learning program suited for the severely—profoundly handicapped. Not only would this program teach the basic principles of horticulture, but it would also teach, in an interesting way, the fundamental concepts applicable to many fields in terms of horticultural skills. Areas that were covered included greenhouse maintenance, plant propagation, physiology, landscaping, plant pathology and identification, different types of gardening, the study of soils, and related skills (commercial aspects), which were all presented on a level that was understandable to the trainees. The horticultural skills that were learned were used as tools to help the trainees become proficient in other areas. The development of fine motor skills is an area of great importance. Taking cuttings, weeding, transplanting seedlings, removing dead leaves, and making flower arrangements all require various degrees of finger dexterity. A variety of gross motor skills is also incorporated in the program. Transferring potted plants from the benches into flats, carrying flats, watering the plants, and sweeping the greenhouse are tasks which are performed daily. The trainees also participate in more strenuous activities such as pushing a loaded wheelbarrow, using a rake or a hoe, and transporting quantities of sand or soil mixtures. A climbing apparatus with three steps on either end is used to water plants purposely set at an elevated level.

Using horticulture as a tool, skills and concepts often taught in a classroom situation are emphasized. The trainees enjoy distinguishing and identifying the various natural colors and color tones found in flowers and other plant parts or that are illustrated in books and catalogs. The color coding of each trainee has been found to be a valuable tool in emphasizing responsibility and organization as well as in teaching colors. For example, each trainee is responsible for the complete care and maintenance of a bench section, a weed basket, a flat, a notebook, and a coat hook, all of which are orange.

A severely-profoundly handicapped individual often learns concepts more quickly through repetition in an everyday living or working environment. Many of these concepts, such as shape and form, have therefore been applied to daily tasks. For example, each shelf or drawer and the tools and equipment belonging there are coded with colored shapes. Therefore, a person knows that the crayon container marked with a green circle belongs on the shelf with the green circle. The various shapes and sizes of hanging tools are also learned when replaced on their outlined forms. And, naturally, we learn the shapes and sizes of various plant parts.

Reading and writing skills are often practiced during the course of the day. Labels are made by the trainees for all plants. These labels are arranged in alphabetical order. Signs such as window, door, poison, pot, and sand are placed on corresponding objects whenever possible. Horticulture books and catalogs are also used as reading materials.

Simple mathematical problems are dealt with throughout the day. For example, if a trainee was transplanting five herbs in two-inch pots, he or she would count out the same number of four-inch pots to put them into. Trainees participate in the inventory of plants each month. This requires counting large numbers of plants.

A favorite activity often used as a reward or a break from a hard day's work is arts and crafts. The trainees enjoy covering a wastebasket with old seed catalogs, making peanut butter and pine cone bird feeders, and painting flats and weeding baskets. A wide variety of skills is incorporated in each of these activities.

An area which is continually emphasized is communication. With the assistance of a speech therapist, individual speech problems are analyzed and concentrated on. A favorite game using various communicative skills is played with a bag containing assorted greenhouse equipment. The trainees must put their hand in the bag and identify the object by touching it. For those more proficient in speech, visitors afford excellent opportunity to give tours of the horticultural program.

It is extremely important for the senses of all individuals to be continually stimulated. Herbs, being our predominant crop, offer an excellent aid in this stimulation. The tastes and smells can be studied individually or can be related to their separate uses; for example, the relationship between mint and gum or between pizza and oregano. Throughout the day, sight and touch are constantly being incorporated in the program.

Several methods are employed to aid the trainees in functioning at a higher level in everyday living situations. Through selling plants to customers, making deliveries, and conducting tours, trainees learn to deal with the public more efficiently. While doing joint projects, trainees are put in situations where it is important to be able to work with others.

Another major goal of the program is to give each person a sense of responsibility. Trainees are assigned individual plants for which they are responsible. This responsibility also aids the trainee in becoming a more self-sufficient individual.

In the future, more advanced skills can be developed. Through working with plants, trainees will better understand various relationships. Complex relationships might be of nature to itself or nature to people. Simpler forms might include a pot's relationship to a plant or to another pot. Trainees will learn how to organize their work efficiently and how to make judgments. At present, the amount of water or where to take cuttings are difficult concepts to grasp. I hope to include personal growth concepts in my program also. This can be taught as the situations arise and through methods of plant propagation.

Many projects have been undertaken in the past six months. Throughout the summer, the other section of the horticulture program was involved with landscaping work. During this time, my program was carried out in the existing greenhouse, continuing the propagation and organization of plants. An herb garden which showed a variety of the herbs grown in our greenhouse was constructed in front of the Apple Doll House Herb Shop. These herbs were also available for sale in the shop. An attractive entrance to the greenhouse was planted as a preview to the many plants for sale within. A one-quarter acre tomato crop was harvested, and those tomatoes which were not used were sold. In the fall, the entire horticulture crew was transported to a nearby apple orchard where we picked up the drops. Throughout the year, nature walks were taken and flowers for drying and other materials were collected. In November, preparations for the Christmas sale were made. Herb sachets and Christmas wreaths were assembled by the trainees and sold along with plants in the greenhouse. In the past six months, these projects and many other smaller ones were accomplished.

A major objective was to design and supervise the construction of a new greenhouse. This would be unique, in that it would be specifically designed for use by the handicapped. The finished product was an accumulation of ideas by the director of SARAH*, Ted Bergeron; the architect, Lombardi and Waldo; the carpenter, Bob Lowry, and his assistant, Mark Schofield; STEM Horticulture Supervisor, Ted Babbitt, and myself. The total dimensions of the greenhouse are 29 by 29 feet with a furnace room 6 by 8 feet. The square shape allows for the staff to supervise from the center as well as making mobility easier for those who are handicapped. The framing is constructed of Douglas fir, hemlock fir, and plywood with the finish lumber being rough-sawn eastern pine. The floor is poured high in the middle so all water runs outward toward the perimeter drainage system of perforate plastic tubing set in gravel. The floor is a four-inch wire-reinforced concrete slab set on gravel. The hip roof has a center vent cupola which is supported by four center posts. Corrugated translucent plexiglass was used

---

*Shoreline Association for the Retarded and Handicapped, Inc.

for windows, with screens in the summer. This variety of windows allows for screening off unpleasant views or distracting activity. The plexiglass is placed for aesthetic purposes. The windows are opened by tipping for added ventilation. The doors, which are 3 feet 6 inches by 6 feet, provide ample room for use by wheelchairs or for moving large items in and out. A ramp leading from the main workshop to the greenhouse and continuing to the parking lot was constructed specifically for the handicapped. The slope is 1 inch in 12 inches to allow for ease in movement up and down. An oil-fired hot water heating system was chosen because of its economical practical value. An additional economical measure was the installment of polyethylene on the ceiling of the greenhouse. During the winter months, the polyethylene serves as insulation. For a more even distribution of heating, an economical high capacity fin and tube baseboard system was chosen. In order to provide adequate ventilation for the greenhouse, a 36 inch exhaust fan was installed in the cupola. It is operated by a two-speed motor connected to a two-stage thermometer with the purpose of maintaining even and gentle cooling of the greenhouse. This system has been programmed to cycle from off to low to high and vice versa according to fluctuations in room temperature. In conjunction with the fan, soffit vents, installed intermittently along the perimeter of the greenhouse, would open and close automatically to facilitate ventilation control. The inside of the greenhouse is as unique a design as the outside structure. Benches are located around most of the perimeter with separate areas for a propagation bench and office space. There were two main considerations taken in designing the benches. The first was that they had to be functional and practical in terms of greenhouse use. The second was that they had to be adopted for use by the trainees. Some handicapped persons, including those in wheelchairs, have a shorter arm span than the average person. Because of this, the benches had to be made 27 inches wide; however, in order to utilize as much space, a 9 inch sliding leaf extension was added to the benches. There is a 1 inch lip on the front of the extension which when pushed in or out prevents water from dripping on a person who may be in a wheelchair. Other special considerations had to be made in terms of designing an adequate drainage system. The benches were built at a slight backward slant to allow for drainage through the crevice formed by two adjoining bench sections. A 4 by 3 feet bottom heated propagation bench was placed on casters for easy mobility to different sections of the greenhouse. When not being used for taking cuttings, it can be conveniently placed in an area between two benches and plugged into a nearby wall socket. Other features of the greenhouse are outdoor electrical outlets, light switches, and control panels all adapted for use by handicapped individuals. The horticultural program participants were able to witness the construction of the new greenhouse while participating in outside activities such as working in the gardens or washing out plastic pots in the sun. Some eager members assisted in the actual construction. When the greenhouse structure was completed, the enthusiasm of the horticultural crew and volunteers about "moving in" was tremendous! Everyone pitched in moving plants, cleaning up, painting, hauling furniture and generally in making the greenhouse a beautiful environment in which to work.

My final objective was to work towards the establishment of a self-sufficient productive horticulture program run primarily by the severely-profoundly handicapped. A number of contracts were made with retail outlets for the purchase of wholesale herb plants. By participating in the actual deliveries and inventories, the trainees witnessed the outcome of the products they had so carefully cultivated. A percentage of all sales was awarded to trainees according to their efforts and participation in the greenhouse. Although the main income was the sale of herbs and specimen plants, other horticulturally related projects were also sold. For example, herb sachets, Christmas wreaths, and dried flower arrangements were displayed in the Gift Shop.

As an active participant in the horticultural program, I have noted that the people involved made considerable progress in several different training areas and have turned out quality products. This, however, is not as important as the therapy involved. Most beneficial are the varied experiences, personal growth, and memorable and enjoyable times shared by volunteers, trainees, and myself while working together. These play an intricate part in the success of any therapeutic program. In the future, we plan to expand the sale of herb plants into a full-scale "herb business." This will provide us with an added activity during the winter of drying and packaging garden grown herbs in quantity. The trainees will also benefit from the added sales experience. We also plan to construct a nature trail suitable for handicapped individuals. This will be located on STEM grounds amidst wooded areas and herb gardens. Trainees will receive instruction in related crafts such as pottery, as well as macrame plant hangers. Vegetable gardens will be planned and cultivated, with the products being sold to STEM food services. I am optimistic that the next year's program will be enlightening and productive for all. Many other spontaneous projects will no doubt surface throughout the year.

Chapter Three

UNDERSTANDING THE DISABLED

HANDICAPPED — A DEFINITION

THE word *handicapped* originated from the Anglo-Saxon phrase *hand-in-the-cap*, an ancient game of chance. One person challenged another for an article in return for something in exchange. Forfeit money was placed in a cap as odds to be awarded along with the article which was of inferior value as determined by a referee. The hand-in-the-cap was a way of insuring equality and encouraging the contest. In time, the phrase was shortened to the word *handicap*, and this word came to be used for persons who were inferior in economic competition because of mental or physical defects. Later, the word was used to describe disadvantages in successful competition for any reason.

The word *handicapped* still refers to the disabled, but now the word is used to describe persons with degrees of differences that are physical, psychological, or social. Everyone is handicapped in one way or another. The degree of misfortune depends upon the element of chance. Any person whose daily activities are restricted or limited may be considered handicapped. An inability to compete successfully in all areas of life labels a person as *handicapped*.

Most handicapped persons are not restricted as much by their actual disability as they are by the effects of their disability upon their personality. The disabled are emotionally limited by feelings of inferiority and depression which wipe out the incentive to be productive. Fear becomes reality when it is known that life will be more difficult and less enjoyable.

The horticultural therapist has a responsibility to see that the disabled have opportunities to experience activities as the normal do and to grow in skills. Personal success in activities adds to a desirable self-image, and one that assists the disabled person toward independence. When a person is disabled in any way, he becomes less capable of participation and more absorbed in his own processes. If this continues, he regresses and becomes unable to participate in other activities. The disabled tend to be egocentric and need outside interests. These interests are increased when the disabled learn to set obtainable goals and to reach success. The therapist must show that one's potential for self-expression and satisfaction makes a handicap unimportant.

The old practice of categorizing individuals according to a specific handicap is phasing out in favor of providing the kind of physical and intellectual atmosphere in which the person can best be helped. To some, the creation of stereotypes through the use of medical labels such as *C.P.'s, spastics, or hemi's* necessitates medically oriented leadership. Experience has shown, however, that a person who uses horticulture for therapy does not need to be medically oriented in order to be successful. In fact, the lack of specific medical knowledge may actually be an advantage.

A person working with the disabled must possess a good knowledge of human personality, its development, and the dynamics of human behavior. One basis for understanding the disabled is to have a clear understanding of ourselves. Dr. Menninger states that most, if not all, persons have specific feelings about the handicapped and react either positively or negatively. Curiosity, pity, oversolicitousness, mild dislike, repugnance, complete rejection, and fear are feelings which are commonly expressed. Curiosity is the most common, and pity is felt when there is a recognition of a condition but no understanding of it.

Early history of the United States shows a neglect of the handicapped. Multiple handicapped persons such as the cerebral palsied were diagnosed as mentally deficient and hopeless and were placed permanently in institutions. It was not until after the twentieth century that changes in attitudes emerged concerning the treatment of all types of disabilities.

The horticultural therapist must not become involved or overly concerned with the medical background of the individuals with whom he is working. It is best to accept and treat these persons as participants in a regular horticultural program. One may consider the limitations of an individual or a group, but the horticultural therapist should not be hampered or confused in his own mind concerning their abilities. Indeed, these so-called limitations are variable and continually changing. A disabled person must be able to express himself naturally through interest or other normal motivation, without worrying about what muscle to move or exercising because it is "good for him." If he knows that the horticultural therapist is dealing with him as a normal person, he is more relaxed as a participant. When the therapist provides the participants with incentives and opportunities to exceed their "limitations," desirable therapy often results.

The following pages describe the physical, emotional, and intellectual characteristics of specific disabilities. It is not intended to be a medical treatise, but a guide to better understanding your patients, clients, or students. Implications for horticultural activities are also discussed. Specific activities are sometimes mentioned for a particular group, but to avoid repetition, the activities are listed in another section and are coded according to their appropriateness for a group.

> "In nature there is no blemish but the mind.
> None can be called deform'd but the unkind."
>
> — Shakespeare

References

Apton, A. 1959. *The Handicapped, A Challenge to the Nonhandicapped.* Citadel Press, New York

Black, E. E. and D. A. Nagel. 1975. *Physically Handicapped Children: A Medical Atlas for Teachers.* Grune & Stratton, New York

Blackwell, R. B. and R. R. Joynt (eds). 1972. *Learning Disabilities Handbook for Teachers.* Thomas, Springfield, Ill.

Bowley, A. H. and L. Gardner. 1972. *Handicapped Child.* Longman, Inc., New York

Chapmen, F. M. 1960. *Recreation Activities for the Handicapped.* Ronald Press, New York

Cobb, A. B. 1973. *Medical and Psychological Aspects of Disability*. American Lecture Series in Social and Rehabilitation Psychology. Publication No. 868. Thomas, Springfield, Ill.
—— — . 1974. *Special Problems in Rehabilitation*. Thomas, Springfield, Ill.
Crain, J. 1974. *Early Childhood Education for Diversely Handicapped Children*. Bureau of Education for the Handicapped, U.S. Office of Education.
Frye, V. and M. Peters. 1972. *Therapeutic Recreation: Its Theory, Philosophy and Practice*. Stackpole Books, Harrisburg, P.
Henderson, P. 1974. *Disability in Childhood and Youth*. Oxford Univ. Press Inc., New York
Hunt, V. V. 1955. *Recreation for the Handicapped*. Prentice-Hall, Inc., New York
Kessler, H. H. 1953. *Rehabilitation of the Physically Handicapped*. Columbia Univ. Press, New York
Michaux, L. A. 1970. *Physically Handicapped and the Community: Some Challenging Breakthroughs*. Thomas, Springfield, Ill.
Mosey, A. C. 1973. *Activities Therapy*. Raven Press, New York
Neff, H. and J. Pilch. 1975. *Teaching Handicapped Children Easily: A Manual for the Average Classroom Teacher without Specialized Teaching*. Thomas, Springfield, Ill.
Rathbone, J. L. and C. Lucas. 1970. *Recreation in Total Rehabilitation*. Thomas, Springfield, Ill.
Robinson, F. M. (ed.). 1974. *Therapeutic Re-Creation: Ideas and Experiences*. Thomas, Springfield, Ill.
Wright, B. 1960. *Physical Disability — A Psychological Approach*. Harper & Row, New York

THE AGED

Gerontology is the study of all aspects of aging. Old age is viewed as a period of declining abilities, and it often brings on handicaps. The effects of old age vary considerably with an individual's temperament and resistance to physical and mental decline.

Physical Characteristics

Physical strength, agility, speed, coordination, and energy decrease gradually, and there are changes in hearing and vision. Frequency of illness is increased in old age. Be aware that old age is not a disease, but the disabilities arising from it are.

Emotional Characteristics

Emotional responses in the aged must be understood in light of their adjustment to problems concerning their changed role in society. Some feel lost, unimportant, and useless. Fear of aging causes much anxiety. They need to be touched and to be cared for. The therapist must be very patient and be a good listener, and, at the same time, converse freely with them.

Intellectual Characteristics

Motivation and interest in new things seems to decrease, and many suffer a loss of memory and recall. This decline in mental ability has its roots in poor work habits coupled with routine activities.

Implications for Horticulture

The aged can experience many healthful benefits from gardening. Moderate exercise and stimulating activity give the aged a new purpose for living. The elderly must have something constructive to do. Older tissue needs stimulation to maintain its efficiency. In most cases, success for the aged is how they make use of their leisure time. Older people can develop their skills for leisure if they have a chance to explore their interests. They will usually enjoy activities that they engaged in when they were young. Activities that have continuity and that sustain interest should comprise much of the program, and those of a hobby nature that encourage latent creativity often bring a tremendous response.

When planning a program in horticulture, consider structuring it on the basis of interest clubs or groups. Participation and not perfection should be emphasized in the program. Let them set up the work area, prepare materials, and assist in other ways. Allow the participants to progress at their own rate. Avoid haste, and work at a slower pace. The leader or therapist should realize that older persons rarely do things to please him. Avoid confusion by not having too many leaders converging on a unit of older people at the same time. They can plan most of the activities and they will carry them out, but they will still need an adviser and individual assistance in some of the activities.

References

Bond, C. A. 1972. *Older Citizens Bring Young Thumbs to a Wide Range of Gardening.* USDA Yearbook of Agriculture, House Doc. No. 29:287-292.

Botwinick, J. 1973. *Aging and Behavior.* Springer Pub., N.Y.

Fish, H. and E. Fish. 1971. *Activities Program for Senior Citizens.* Prentice-Hall, Englewood Cliffs, N. J.

Gould, E. and L. Gould. 1971. *Crafts for the Elderly.* Thomas, Springfield, Ill.

Horne, D. C. 1974. *An Evaluation of the Effectiveness of Horticultural Therapy on the Life Satisfaction Level of Aged Persons Confined to a Rest Care Facility.* M. S. Thesis, Clemson University, Clemson, S. C.

Long, J. 1974. *Caring For and Caring About Elderly People: A Guide to the Rehabilitative Approach.* J. B. Lippincott Co., New York

Merril, T. 1975. *Activities for the Aged and Infirm: A Handbook for the Untrained Worker.* Thomas, Springfield, Ill.

THE ALCOHOLIC

At the present time, alcoholism is listed as the nation's third leading health problem, second only to mental illness and cardiovascular diseases. In 1955, the estimated number of alcoholics in the United States was approximately five million. In 1965, a statistical survey published by the National Council on Alcoholism approximated a figure of six million. In 1971, the National Institute on Alcohol Abuse and Alcoholism estimated the number at nine million. Today, there are over ten million alcoholics in the United States.

Alcoholism is an extremely complex problem with cultural, psychological, physiological, and even spiritual overtones. It is difficult to assign any particular personality characteristics to the alcoholic, but, in general, they are unable to endure much anxiety or frustration, they are very sensitive, they often feel isolated, and they tend to act impulsively.

Implications for Horticulture

Alcoholics Anonymous groups have shown that recovery is possible for the person who is handicapped by alcoholism. Treatment involves a great deal of time, energy, and personal relationships. In working with the alcoholic, warmth, genuineness, acceptance, caring, and trustworthiness are necessary. The attitude of the therapist is very important. The alcoholic is a sick person suffering from a disease. The alcoholic needs someone who understands how he feels and who gives affection and encouragement. Group psychotherapy has been the most effective, but a multidisciplinary approach for the treatment of alcoholism is being emphasized. A diversified program with alternatives for the participants seems to be the most successful. At the present time, horticulture is useful in an adjunctive way for relaxation and anxiety reduction.

For the alcoholic, horticultural activity offers the following therapeutic values:

1. It offers well-structured tasks with both immediate and long-term gratifications.
2. It offers opportunity to cope with objective realities.
3. It appeals to the senses, reaffirming the whole person.
4. It emphasizes the organic and biological processes of man and his surroundings in contrast to mechanical, produced processes and goods.
5. It reduces stress through social interaction.

References

Babow, I. 1973. "The need for variety in treatment programs." *Alcohol Health and Research World* 1: 12-13.

Blum, E. M. and R. H. Blum. 1967. *Alcoholism: Modern Psychological Approaches to Treatment.* Jossey-Bass, San Francisco, Ca.

Catanzaro, R. J. (ed.). 1974. *Alcoholism: The Total Treatment Approach.* Thomas, Springfield, Ill.

Clinebell, H. J. 1968. *Understanding the Alcoholic.* Abingdon Press, Nashville, Tenn.

Cobb A. B. 1974. *Special Problems in Rehabilitation.* Thomas, Springfield, Ill.

Fox, R. 1968. "A Multidisciplinary approach to the treatment of alcoholism." *Inter. J. Psychiatry* 5(1):34-38.

Oakley, S. R. 1972. "The role of recreation in alcoholic rehabilitation". *In* M. N. and C. R. Hormachea (ed.). *Recreation in Modern Society.* Holbrood Press, Boston, M.

Stein, A. 1972. "Group therapy with alcoholics." *In* H. J. Kaplan and B. J. Sadock (ed.). *Groups and Drugs.* E. P. Dutton, N. Y.

THE BLIND

The legally blind are those with visual acuity of 20/200 or less with the aid of glasses. However, most of those classified as blind have some useful sight and may recognize perception of form, movement, or light. Infectious diseases such as measles, scarlet fever, typhoid fever, and smallpox cause the most blindness. Other causes are accidents, diabetes, vascular diseases, corneal scars, cataracts, and glaucoma.

Physical Characteristics

Growth and maturation are somewhat retarded, and some may lack physical vitality. The blind become skilled in interpreting auditory, tactile, and kinesthetic sensations. Teachers of the blind stress that with right-handed persons, the right hand is the more dominant motor hand, whereas the left hand is more sensitive and is used for reading Braille and for feeling objects. The blind have fewer facial expressions, and it is sometimes difficult to interpret their mood.

Emotional Characteristics

The blind tend to be frustrated, egocentric, and may lack initiative. However, some are very initiative. Blind children tend to withdraw, fantasize, and are less competitive. Adults are anxious about the future and have fears of social inadequacy.

They may be despondent, dependent, or withdrawn. The blind adolescent has to come to terms with the situation and adjusted to the demands of a sighted, competitive world. Some will regress, become stubborn, abusive, and even destructive.

Intellectual Characteristics

Many are of good intelligence, capable of learning Braille and other skills, but they differ in capacity just as sighted individuals. They need more conversation about objects because experience is restricted by lack of visual information.

Implications for Horticulture

Many stimulating experiences are needed if the blind and the visually handicapped are to develop to their maximum capacity. Nature activities are very stimulating for the blind. The trees, wind, rain, and sunrise have feeling qualities that are exciting. The blind need tactile experiences. Make use of natural materials such as acorns, sticks, leaves, and fruits. Many are eager to touch a branch, feel the texture of bark, and hear the sound of a birdcall. Let them feel the soil. Flowers fascinate the blind as do fragrant herbs, shrubs, and trees. They learn about objects by touch, smell, and taste. Try to emphasize texture, size, smell, and sound. The blind literally learn through their fingers, and they can sort out materials with great concentration for long periods of time. At first, their motor coordination may be jerky and uncontrolled, and holding an object may be difficult.

Use simple procedures and be aware of increasing tensions. Increased random movements, or unaccounted-for silences are indicative of growing tensions. If this occurs, change the pace of the activity. The word *see* should be used in giving instructions because the word also implies an understanding. They need the security of knowing where the leader is and what is happening during the activity. Praise, patience, and precision are necessary.

The blind can be creative by working with clay, sand, and other media. They feel at ease with materials that they can mold and shape. Making planters is very successful. Planting, growing, and "observing" a plant can become a fascinating visual sequencing activity for the blind. A plant's growth is recorded from week to week over a six-week period. To reinforce this task, an additional plant or seed is planted each week so that upon completion of the activity, there are various stages of plant growth that can be compared. This kind of activity provides the opportunity to scrutinize a natural phenomenon and note small changes over a period of time.

When working outdoors, soil surfaces of different compositions help give them orientation. In the garden, horizontal ropes or "kick rails" at ankle heights with knots at various intervals are very helpful. A kick rail is usually placed eight to twelve inches above the ground so that it can be contacted by the ankle or with a cane. In this way, the blind can become familiar with the area as to size, shape, and composition. They should handle tools and equipment, and these should be stored in the same location to prevent any confusion. To aid in planting, place large rings on the ground, and have them plant within the rings.

Concerning special gardens for the blind, the American Foundation for the Blind believes that the establishment of special gardens is not in their best interests. The Foundation points out that such gardens foster stereotypes that may carry a psychological impact that is distasteful to the blind. They recommend that such facilities be available to all persons and not designated for the enjoyment of one special group. Likewise, the Blind Veterans Association suggests that blind individuals can be served much better by being provided with special methods of horticulture that would enable them to carry on gardening activities independently. In addition, a Forest Service Manual emphasizes that the physically handicapped wish to be included in the mainstream of life without an inordinate amount of special or segregated facilities and programs.

For the blind person with a sincere interest in horticulture, there is great potential for vocational training. There are many jobs in the horticultural industry that visually handicapped individuals can do. These include the production, marketing, and utilization of fruits, vegetables, flowers, ornamental, and processed products. For example, commercial growers of bedding plants need employees to systematically fill large numbers of seed flats with soil, and then plant seed in them. Such stationary assignments can easily be taught to the blind. Those with partial sight have even more potential. There is the possibility of starting a small greenhouse business which deals in bedding plants, vegetable seedlings, and rooted cuttings that can be sold locally.

The world of nature and plant growth is very significant to the blind. During a nature walk at the Bartlett Arboretum, a blind individual expressed his impressions by saying, "I like the scent and the quiet here." "You know, even without sight, you get a feeling of green." Another blind individual expressed her delight for the beautiful yellow roses. "How did you know they were yellow?" I asked. "I smelled them," she said, "yellow roses have a stronger scent than other roses!"

References

Anonymous. 1972. "Nature trail for the blind." *Horticulture* 50(8): 1.

Bishop, V. E. 1971. *Teaching the Visually Limited Child*. Thomas, Springfield, Ill.

Bluhm, D. L. 1968. *Teaching the Retarded Visually Handicapped: Indeed They are Children*. W. B. G. Saunders, Philadelphia, P.

Burgess, L. 1967. "Fragrance gardens for the blind — fact or fiction?" *Amer. Hort. Mag.* 46(1): 25-28

Floyd, J. A., Jr. and T. L. Senn. "An investigation into the physical and psychological response of the visually handicapped to some selected woody and herbaceous plant material." *Tech. Bul. 1045, S. C. Agric. Expt. Sta.*, Clemson Univ., Clemson, S. C.

Garvey, J. M. 1969. "Touch and see: nature trail at the aboretum, Washington, D. C." *Parks and Rec.* 4: 20-22

McEachern, M. 1970. "Beauty is not in the eyes of these beholders." *Today's Health* 48: 79-80.

Perelman, B. 1975. *Braille*. Ithaca House, Berkeley, C.

THE CARDIAC

Specialists recognize about twenty causes for heart disease including rheumatic fever, commonly occurring in childhood; high blood pressure or hypertension, affecting both young and old adults; and coronary heart disease, including coronary thrombosis and coronary arteriosclerosis which are most prevalent in middle and old age.

It is commonly believed that a person suffering from heart disease is destined to a life of inactivity. This is far from true. The majority live active lives, and roughly 70 to 80 percent return to some kind of work.

Physical Characteristics

Children are often too active and adults are too sedentary. Damage to the dominant hemisphere of the brain results in aphasia or loss of verbal skills. Damage to the nondominant hemisphere of the brain results in loss of visuomotor skills. Hearing may also be impaired. Hemiplegics and stroke patients vary in their functional impairment from that of the bedridden to those with almost complete self-sufficiency.

Emotional Characteristics

Most experience some kind of anxiety. Some become antisocial and uncooperative, whereas others use the defense mechanism of denial. Some cannot control their emotions, and tend to cry, laugh, or to be irritable. Defeatest attitudes, the inability to accept restrictions, and compulsive drives often appear in cardiac children.

Intellectual Characteristics

There may be a change in memory, judgment, ability to think abstractly, and ability to shift from one task to another. Hemiplegics make errors in judging foreground and background, vertical and horizontal because of visual-perceptual problems.

Implications for Horticulture

The therapist should first consult a physician concerning the physical capabilities of an individual, and then plan a horticultural program accordingly. The strenuousness of various gardening activities is determined not by the activity, but by how it is done. Avoid static-held positions, quick movements, lifting heavy objects, strong competition, prolonged activities, and high or low temperatures. Encourage good body mechanics such as bending at the knees rather than at the waist. Work should be done at a good sitting height using tall stools at tables so that the person works "downhill" rather than "uphill." Those with visual and auditory impairments must also be taken into consideration. Some will require verbal instructions whereas others will require demonstrations. Plan to teach only one activity per session because some may have difficulty in changing tasks. With minor modifications, the normal play experiences can be enjoyed by most cardiac children. When doing strenuous activities, be aware of body symptoms such as shortness of breath, pain, dizziness, and fatigue. Encourage rest periods when necessary, and try not to hurry through an activity.

References

Zankel, H. T. 1971. *Stroke Rehabilitation: A Guide to the Rehabilitation of an Adult Patient Following a Stroke*. Thomas, Springfield, Ill.
Zohman, L. R. and J. S. Tobias. 1970. *Cardiac Rehabilitation*. Grune & Stratton, New York

THE CONVALESCENT AND THE HOMEBOUND

The convalescent describes a person involved in a progressive state of recovery toward normalcy. Most are bedridden and are restricted in their activities. In the case of the homebound, many may be chronically ill, but those in rest homes may not be.

Physical Characteristics

In addition to the disability, if one exists, metabolism drops, appetite lessens, and muscle strength decreases.

Emotional Characteristics

The convalescing child is very anxious. Some children feel guilty about their illness and think they are being punished. If they are institutionalized for long periods, they may become passive, unresponsive, and frustrated. Adults experience a major change in their patterns of life. They may become ego-centric, apathetic, dependent, and insecure. Some are overde-pendent, deny their symptoms, exaggerate their symptoms, show hostility, or become very manipulative. In many cases, homebound persons are in the lower strata of economic pro-ductivity and are often faced with inappropriate housing and transportation problems. These conditions in addition to the disability cause emotional distress and withdrawal.

Implications for Horticulture

The therapist should be aware that the approach must be varied depending on the particular situation. Basically, the therapist should relax his clients and provide an atmosphere for anticipation. Boredom and self-centeredness must be re-placed with interesting things to do and to think about. Children and adolescents need to continue to learn, and adults need to fill their hours with enjoyment. Patients confined in-doors often derive great pleasure from thoughts and activities that take them outdoors or bring the outdoors in to them.

Programs do not need special or elaborate equipment. Paper bags can be pinned to mattresses to hold supplies. The thera-pist can also use a push cart. Large cardboard boxes with two sides removed make good bed tables. Old sheets or large plastic sheets can be used to protect the bedding. Try to use light-weight containers and tools.

For long-term patients, start a garden club with a program consisting of month to month activities. Invite speakers from time to time, decorate the hospital on special holidays, and make arrangements for other patients. Use a portable green-house or garden under lights. Show colored slides of flowers, gardens, and parks. Kitchen gardening and herb growing are very popular. To increase social contacts for homebound pa-tients, start a garden club and communicate with a newsletter.

The therapist's warmth and willingness to give friendship are often more important than the content of the horticultural program. Much of the program may be carried on by volunteers who bring fresh faces, enthusiasm, and invaluable skills.

Happiness Helps Recovery

References

Rich, M. K. 1960. *Handicrafts for the Homebound Handicapped.* Thomas, Springfield, Ill.
Scully, A. 1969. *Fun in Bed.* Simon & Schuster, Inc., New York

THE DEAF

Deafness may range from mild to marginal, moderate, severe, or profound. It may be caused by injury, infections, anomalies, tumors, and degeneration such as aging, arteriosclerosis, and diabetes.

The world to the deaf is silent, and this tends to induce a sense of isolation. The background noises of everyday living that are important psychologically are absent, and life is liter-ally full of surprises, for things may happen very suddenly without warning.

Physical Characteristics

Most deaf persons are physically sound and are normal in their general motor ability. Some are inaccurate in recognizing space and motion, and they can be easily distracted by the movement of others. Their tension level is often high. Because they compensate through sight, the eyes are often fatigued. Children sometimes display many unpurposeful movements due to residual tensions.

Emotional Characteristics

The young are fearful and anxious, and depression is common in adults. As a group, the deaf are less aggressive and tend to avoid their environment. Social maturity of the deaf child is retarded, especially when the parents are overindulgent. This delayed maturity is most noticeable in adolescence, often resulting in antisocial behavior. Some do not understand humor since it is a play on words.

In general, the effects of deafness upon the personality are different and are dependent upon when the deafness occurred. There are many emotional effects of deafness upon a person in his efforts toward self-adjustment. These emotional effects may produce no personality disturbances at all, or they may create more handicaps than the actual hearing loss.

Intellectual Characteristics

There are no mental limitations, but without language development, the deaf are lacking one major tool for thought. Mental retardation becomes a problem especially with children who have been cut off from necessary learning experiences. The therapist must provide constructive activities to foster intellectual development.

Implications for Horticulture

Many can read, write, and also read lips. Speech is not essential if the activities are demonstrated. Dr. Betty Miller of Gallaudet College believes that there is too much emphasis on teaching speech and lipreading; deaf learners do not grow in their own right by making use of their own visual and tactile abilities but instead imitate hearing people. She believes that a combination of art and sign language can help the deaf express themselves both artistically and psychologically.

The deaf seem to avoid anything new because they fear that they cannot follow instructions. They are highly visually oriented, and manual skills such as flower arranging are readily learned. Consideration should be given to the organizational plan of the activities. Experience has shown that the deaf work better in groups than with individual projects. There should be a consistent routine, and the same therapist should be present at each session. Great confusion results if a leader changes his approach or routine and also if a piece of equipment is altered. The situation may become noisy if it is disorganized. Try to give simple, step-by-step directions, and if directions are given verbally, use simple, uncomplicated sentences. Be aware that one individual may be severely regressed to the extent that he needs a great deal of assistance, whereas another individual may need very little assistance.

References

Furth, H. G. 1973. *Deafness and Learning: A Psycho-social Approach.* Wadsworth Pub. Co. Inc., Belmont, C

Katz, L., S. L. Mathis, E. C. Merril. 1974. *Deaf Child in the Public Schools.* Interstate Pubs., Danville, Ill.

Wright, D. 1975. *Deafness.* Stein & Day, Inc., New York

THE DRUG ABUSER

Man has been using drugs since ancient times as a means for easing his discomforts and enhancing his pleasures. The drug user is unable to cope with many of the tensions and frustrations that are prevalent in today's society. Drugs, like alcohol, often appear to offer a way out. For some, drugs become a device for stimulation by increasing one's sensitivity. For others, the drug depresses the internal experience of one's self. The drug addict's entire world consists of drugs and the euphoria they provide. Suddenly, the drug takes over and the addict loses control. By the time he reaches the rehabilitation stage, his world has totally disintegrated.

The treatment and rehabilitation of addicts and their return to society is not easy, and it requires intensive work for a long period of time. Rehabilitation demands a broad spectrum of services in personal, social, vocational, and recreational areas. The main purpose of therapy is to help the drug abuser establish himself in a meaningful and supporting role in society. Recovery is based on self-help with the support and concern of others. Feedback from counselors, therapists, and especially from his own peer group helps the addict discover his competency to handle situations, cope with stress, and solve problems. He thus becomes aware of his weaknesses and strengths.

Emotional Characteristics

Although drug abusers vary in their personalities, most suffer from chronic and severe emotional distress prior to use. They experience depression, distrust, hopelessness, guilt, anxiety, anger, interpersonal inhibition, pain, and pleasure. They have feelings of self-devaluation and an inability to compete socially, and they often feel alienated and feel the need for a personal identity.

Implications for Horticulture

The role of the therapist is to direct the person's interests toward activities that have a good chance for success. This requires the ability to motivate the addict. The therapist must have the attitude that he is truly interested in knowing what drugs mean to the abuser. However, the therapist should not overidentify and accept the abusers' rationalizations and should try not to relate to them by using their "hip" language. In part, it means helping the addict develop better language skills and making him feel comfortable using these skills. The dependability and punctuality of the therapist also tell the drug abuser that you are serious and that you are concerned for his rehabilitation.

Activities in horticulture can provide another environment in which the addict can interact. The activity group can be considered to be a personal growth group based on the approach of support and permission with the initiative left basically to the group members. In this situation, the horticultural therapist does not always play an active role.

For the addict who has in the past rarely experienced success, an activity that helps to strengthen one's self-concept and sense of achievement is very important. A flower arrangement can strengthen the appreciation for beauty and creativity. It can result in self-esteem, and also the esteem of others. It can foster the feeling of tenderness for those who have experienced much aggression in the past.

A resident at New Hope Manor in New York, a live-in therapeutic community for young, female drug addicts, expresses the significance of working with plants in this way: "watching the ways of plants, a girl can learn of a life respectable to herself. To be able to view the sun-color yellow of the sunflower, the way it reaches its head to the sky." A participant of the Manhattan Psychiatric Center's Horticultural Sciences Project responds in this way: "For the first time, I'm doing something and I'm learning which I didn't think I could do before. I feel like I've grown. I had a very low esteem of myself. But now I'm blooming just like the way my plants bloom."

References

Berry, J. S. 1975. "A hortitherapy program for substance abusers." *Research Series No. 156, S. C. Agric. Expt. Sta.*, Clemson Univ., Clemson, S. C.

Kolber, P. 1972. *Rehabilitation of the Drug Abuser.* The Clearing House, Rehabilitation Training Program, Oklahoma State University

Zinberg, N. E. and J. A. Robertson. 1972. *Drugs and the Public.* Simon & Schuster, New York

THE EMOTIONALLY DISABLED

The National Committee against Mental Illness estimates that about one in every ten persons is suffering from some form of mental illness. The general term, *insanity,* has been replaced with terms such as mental illness, psychoses, and psychoneuroses to cover a vast array of types, degrees, and causes of emotional disturbances.

Many neuroses and psychoses result from social problems that place the individual under stress, making adjustment very difficult or impossible. Emotionally disturbed people are those who are socially misdirected in their relations with others.

Physical Characteristics

Physical motions may be either hyperactive or hypoactive. Some exhibit grimacing, postural oddities, and muscle tensions. Others stare into space, an example of catatonic immobility. Psychosomatic illnesses are also exhibited. Treatment or therapy involves physical-chemical alteration involving drugs, shock, or surgery, changes in the environment, and changes in communication.

Emotional Characteristics

Emotional responses are often unrealistic. Psychotics have delusions or obsessions of grandeur, persecution or self-accusation. They tend to misinterpret sensory impulses and stimuli and to experience illusions and hallucinations, and also tend to over- or under-react. Schizophrenia accounts for the highest incidence of all psychoses, and it is characterized by a split between thought and feeling, an escape from reality, and an avoidance of the environment and people. The manic-depressive tends to escape into reality and become overly extroverted with manic stages alternating with depressive stages. Neurotics tend to be anxious about generalities and unknowns. They develop impairments of the senses not physically or neurally based, and exhibit obsession, compulsions, and phobias. People with personality disorders possess emotional instability, often reacting with excitability in everyday stress situations. They may behave either aggressively by being irritable, by throwing tantrums, or by being destructive, or passively by exhibiting helplessness, indecisiveness, or disguised aggressiveness such as procrastination, stubbornness, or childlike pouting.

Intellectual Characteristics

Intelligence is often average or frequently above average, but it is rarely used to its potential.

Implications for Horticulture

Various group activities are favored to encourage interaction with others. Identification with a group creates a pressure to conform. Group activities should be emotionally releasing, emotionally curbing, and emotionally self-gratifying. Success results in security. An activity that allows a patient to regress acceptably may allow him to experience pleasurable emotions connected with his childhood.

Motivation is the greatest problem, but stimulation was found to come more easily from a situation where many opportunities were available, and the patient could choose the activities for himself. For emotionally disturbed children, the setting of a garden helps to release tension. In the words of Dr. James McHugh, attending psychiatrist at Pontiac State Hospital in Michigan, "these children are digging their troubles into the soil."

References

Despert, J. L. 1970. *Emotionally Disturbed Child*. Doubleday & Co., Inc., New York

Haring, N. G. and E. L. Phillips. 1962. *Educating Emotionally Disturbed Children*. McGraw-Hill Book Co., New York

Jenkins, R. L. and E. Harms (eds.). 1975. *Understanding Disturbed Children*. Spec. Child Pubns., Seattle, Wa.

THE EPILEPTIC

Epilepsy is a neurological disorder involving a disfunctioning of the brain-regulating mechanisms with reoccurrence of unconsciousness with or without convulsions.

Physical Characteristics

None are present except the seizures. Treatment includes anticonvulsive medication, special diets, education, psychotherapy, and sometimes surgery.

Emotional Characteristics

There are no specific personality traits. Their primary handicap is social. Epileptics fear social rejection because of their condition. Employment is sometimes restricted, some schools exclude them, and some cannot drive cars or do mechanical work for risk of injury.

Intellectual Characteristics

They show extremes of being very bright to being very dull with the majority near average.

Implications for Horticulture

Many physicians recommend strenuous activities and physical work. Seizures are less frequent in those who are active. A program in horticulture should combine active and intellectual activities with social participation. Gardening activities are excellent because they are active, out of doors, and social. Activities with strong emotional or sensory appeal such as landscape gardening and pruning bring favorable emotional responses. It is suggested that more highly technical horticultural activities be used with this group.

References

Epilepsy Foundation of America. 1975. *Epilepsy Rehabilitation*. Little, Brown & Co., Waltham, M.

THE MENTALLY RETARDED

Mental retardation refers to below average intellectual functioning associated with impairment in one or more of the following areas: (1) maturation; (2) learning; and (3) social adjustment. Four social-psychological categories of mental retardation are recognized: mild, moderate, severe, and profound. The mildly retarded can develop social and communicative skills and are not distinguished from the norm until a later age. The moderately retarded can communicate, but have poor social awareness. The severely retarded have poor motor development and minimal speech. The profoundly retarded have gross retardation with a minimal capacity for functioning in sensori-motor areas.

Physical Characteristics

In general, they lack physical coordination. Hearing, speech, sight, and sensory perceptions are inferior. Mongoloids have almond-shaped eyes, a flattened occiput, and a depressed nasal bridge.

Emotional Characteristics

They are impatient and lose interest when goals are out of their reach. Emotional stability is lacking, and they may respond with fear and aggression. The average mongoloid is happy, friendly, and affectionate. Because of continued failure and frustration, the retarded build elaborate defense mechanisms which result in apathy. These defenses can be reduced by activities that provide for successful experiences reinforced with praise.

Intellectual Characteristics

The educational classification according to the Stanford-Binet test divides individuals with low intelligence into four groups: (1) the slow learner (IQ 80-90); (2) the educable mentally retarded (IQ 50-55 to 75-70); (3) the trainable mentally retarded (IQ 30-35 to 50-55); (4) the totally dependent or profoundly mentally retarded (IQ 25-30). The educables are able to achieve in academic subjects at a minimal level, to adjust socially to a point where they can function independently in the community, and to develop occupational adequacies to a degree so that they can support themselves partially or totally at the adult level. The trainable individual has the potential to learn self-help skills, social adjustment, and economic usefulness in the home, in a residential school, or in a sheltered workshop. The educable exhibit difficulty in attention span, recall, transfer, conceptualization, and symbolization. The manipulation of concrete materials should be encouraged. Visual-motor coordination can improve as these skills are used.

Implications for Horticulture

A horticultural program can provide instruction in areas such as academic skills, avocational skills, socialization skills, and vocational skills. The primary objective of the program is to help the individual attain his highest potential and to adjust to his environment.

An emphasis should be placed upon cooperation in groups. Groups should be organized on the basis of both mental and chronological age. Mental age is the most important factor in determining interest. The groups should be limited to 5 or 6 persons, and the sessions should be short (15-30 minutes). The activity should be repeated from session to session to regain the participants' interest and memory. The content and materials of the activity should be kept simple with short sequential stops in between. Slow, direct instructions should accompany demonstrations, and verbal instruction should be kept to a minimum. The activities should be designed so that there will always be some success. Avoid long-term projects because of the short attention span of the mentally retarded.

Aggressive drives can be directed by digging in the garden. The mentally retarded enjoy colorful plants, slides, and pictures, making macrame hangers, planters, and terrariums, and greenhouse tasks are very successful. Maintenance of the greenhouse including such tasks as fertilizing, mixing soil, pruning, stacking pots, watering, and weeding helps to improve physical development including eye and hand coordination. Even though these tasks appear simple, some supervision is still necessary. Horticulturally related activities such as dried flower arrangements, seed mosaics, and pressed flower pictures are also successful.

References

Cruickshank, W. and G. O. Johnson. 1967. *Education of Exceptional Children and Youth.* Prentice-Hall, Inc., Englewood Cliffs, N. J.

Hefley, P. D. 1972. *An Investigation of Horticulture as a Technique for the Rehabilitation of the Older Institutionalized Mentally Retarded Individual.* M. S. Dissertation, Univ. of Maryland, College Park

Hiott, J. A. 1975. "A hortitherapy program for the mentally handicapped." *Research Series No. 157, S. C. Agric. Expt. Sta.,* Clemson Univ., Clemson, S. C.

Kirk, S. A. 1972. *Educating Exceptional Children.* Houghton Mifflin Co., Boston, M.

Kolstoe, O. P. 1970. *Teaching Educable Mentally Retarded Children.* Holt, Rinehart, and Winston, Inc., New York

U. S. Department of Health, Education and Welfare. *Horticulture: An Exceptional Training Medium for Mentally Retarded Females.* Demonstration Grant No. Rd-12-P-55109/3-03.

THE NEUROLOGICALLY DISABLED

The condition known as cerebral palsy involves the impairment of loss of neural activity caused by the lack of formation, malformation, or injury to the brain either before, during, or after birth. It may also result from encephalitis, cerebral hemorrhage, meningitis, or accidents. The five general types are spastic, athetoid, ataxic, tremor, and rigidity.

Spastic: Movements are stiff and jerky. There is a tendency to drool and to have defective speech.

Athetoid: Movements are exaggerated. There are displays of involuntary movements usually with a twisting, rolling motion which is continuous and slow.

Ataxic: There is a disturbed equilibrium and coordination resulting in slurred speech.

Tremor: Rhythmic involuntary contractions are limited to certain muscle groups.

Rigidity: There is almost constant rigidity in certain muscle groups.

Physical Characteristics

The primary characteristic is loss of control over the voluntary muscles. The impairment may be isolated, but usually a variety of combinations occurs. Cerebral palsy is actually a multiple handicap. Some are deaf or have vision problems. Some have trouble with drooling, grimacing, speech, and disorders of digestion. Some are convulsive and fatigue easily. In general, they are restricted in manipulating objects.

Emotional Characteristics

Many cerebral palsied persons are frustrated by their inability to solve the physical, intellectual, and social problems that confront them. They often feel inferior, and they may become aggressive, infantile, or negative. Social rejection causes the most frustration.

Intellectual Characteristics

Some of the cerebral palsied are normal in intelligence, but perceptual impairments cause learning problems, and this necessitates the use of special teaching methods and materials.

Implications for Horticulture

Children need manipulative experiences, whereas adolescents and adults need physically oriented experiences. Both need to belong to social groups. Realistic goals in the horticultural program will provide for emotional satisfaction. Creative experiences should be exploratory. The activities should have prestige value. The cerebral palsied tend to respond best to activities after short periods of rest. Activities that demand free movements are more relaxing than those that require finely coordinated movements. Moderately slow activities such as potting and planting are very successful. The cerebral palsied can perform simple repetitive movements more easily than movements involving many complex changes. They often have difficulty in grasping things, and they can be expected to drop or spill things. Provide additional equipment and materials, and add special adaptations so that equipment can be used successfully. A special lapboard or chair board can be made to fit conveniently over a wheelchair. Some persons can work in a standing position, and it is helpful to use stand-up tables. Encourage them to do things for themselves.

When teaching new activity skills, emphasize the total act rather than its parts so that the motivation to accomplish a task places attention upon the thing to be done rather than upon the act of doing. The participants' attention should be directed to completing a task rather than to holding their bodies in a certain position. For example, they should be taught to concentrate on where a seed or bulb should be placed rather than upon the act of putting it there.

References

Blencowe, S. M. 1969. *Cerebral Palsy and the Young Child.* Longman, Inc., New York

Keats, S. 1973. *Cerebral Palsy.* Thomas, Springfield, Ill.

Marks, N. C. 1974. *Cerebral Palsied and Learning Disabled Children: A Handbook Guide to Treatment, Rehabilitation and Education.* Thomas, Springfield, Ill.

National Easter Seal Society for Crippled Children and Adults. 1950. *A Manual of Cerebral Palsy Equipment.* The Society, Chicago, Ill.

THE ORTHOPEDICALLY DISABLED

Persons that are orthopedically disabled are those commonly thought of as *crippled.* They may be classified in the following way:

Congenital: Those with dislocated hips and arms, spina bifida, club feet, or scoliosis.

Traumatic: Those with hemiplegia, paraplegia, quadriplegia, amputation, or peripheral nerve injury.

Infectious: Those with osteomyelitis, poliomyelitis, or tuberculosis of the bones.

Osteochondritic and nutritional: Those with Perthes disease or epiphysitis.

Metabolic: Those with muscular dystrophy or myasthenia gravis.

Physical Characteristics

Motor performance is slower, less free, and uncoordinated. Balance is poor, and there is less tolerance to fatigue. There are specific movement problems related to the specific disability. Unstable joints must be protected from undue strain, and weakened muscles must not be strained.

Emotional Characteristics

Doctor Joan L. Bardach of the New York Institute for Rehabilitation Medicine states that physically disabled individuals experience emotional and psychological difficulties that arise from three sources: (1) from the physical disability itself; (2) from attitudes of rejection imposed by the society; and (3) from the individual's own emotional reactions to his disability.

The location of the impairment and the cosmetic appearance are psychologically significant. Feelings of personal inferiority, lack of initiative, and timidity are common. Physical disabilities interfere with a person's intellectual, emotional, and social development.

Intellectual Characteristics

Physically, the orthopedically disabled have lost a percentage of their function, but they have retained their mental ability unless their physical condition causes undue psychological trauma. Many have returned to schools and colleges with tremendous success.

Implications for Horticulture

Horticultural activities can be used to lessen some of the emotional difficulties that the physically disabled experience. Stimulation of an interest in horticulture offers an opportunity to interact with others on a basis other than the disability. With success through achievement, the disabled individual can gain confidence which will help him to become active in society again.

Basically, the needs of the physically disabled are not different from those of the nondisabled. Physical movements are the principal outlet for their excess energy and tensions. Equipment and facilities can be designed to assist them in participating in most horticultural activities.

The importance of horticulture for the orthopedically disabled is best described by Doctor Bardach: "Disabled individuals frequently regard the disabled part of themselves as dead. In contrast with handicrafts, involvement in horticulture means involvement in an ongoing, living activity in contradistinction to concern with pessimism, disease and death, and so horticultural therapy can serve to place emphasis on optimism, beauty and life."

References

Ashley, I. E., Jr. 1968. *Analysis of Opportunities for Paraplegics in Certain Ornamental Horticulture Occupations.* Doctoral Dissertation, Univ. of Illinois, Urbana

Bardach, J. L. 1975. "Horticultural therapy for some psychological conditions of the physically disabled." *NCTRH Newsletter:* September.

Frost, A. and R. Frost. 1951. *Handbook for Paraplegics and Quadriplegics.* The Printmark Co., New York

Zankel, H. T. 1971. *Stroke Rehabilitation: A Guide to the Rehabilitation of an Adult Patient Following a Stroke.* Thomas, Springfield, Ill.

Chapter Four

UNDERSTANDING THE DISADVANTAGED

THE disadvantaged are those segments of our society that are alienated due to ethnic and socioeconomic circumstances. They live in the inner city, in the ghetto, in the barrio, on the reservation, and in rural, depressed areas. They are Mexican-Americans, Puerto Ricans, blacks, and rural European immigrants who are not absorbed into society. A large percentage live in substandard housing where children are exposed to health hazards, and limited health care results in a shorter life expectancy. The environment is cruel and difficult with high crime and unemployment rates. The children are confronted with substandard and overcrowded educational facilities with minimal cultural or recreational programs. The behavior of disadvantaged children is often set by parents who are themselves alienated from society. These children are victims of an environment that does not meet their basic needs. In a true sense, they are "handicapped" emotionally, intellectually, and socially. The problem may be compounded even more when they are physically disabled.

Physical Characteristics

Some of the disadvantaged have health problems due to undernourishment. Poor hygiene results in dental problems causing children to be irritable. Prenatal and postnatal care are often lacking, and brain damage and neurological problems result. Many have uncorrected hearing and vision problems. In many cases, the disadvantaged tend to accept their physical discomforts and limitations as a way of life.

Emotional Characteristics

Because of his physical appearance and economic background, the disadvantaged child feels inadequate. He often has a negative self-concept and lacks a personal identity. He may view himself as unsuccessful and unimportant. Stress and frustration result in antisocial behavior and delinquency, or regression and withdrawal into a world of fantasy.

Intellectual Characteristics

The lack of suitable learning experiences causes the disadvantaged child to be easily frightened and frustrated by simple problems. The child is often bored with school and a curriculum that has no relevance to his life or culture. In general, he lacks motivation to achieve success educationally, socially, economically, or occupationally.

Implications for Horticulture

Horticultural activities in disadvantaged areas can have profound psychological effects. Projects such as those conducted by the New York City Housing Authority and Philadelphia's Window-box Program have enabled people to discover new experiences in their own immediate environment.

In general, a horticultural program for the disadvantaged should be a positive, growth-oriented one with an overemphasis on success. This feeling of success and accomplishment is very important to the disadvantaged child who has often suffered many disappointments and failures. There is a need for ego building and for a sense of status and pride. A disadvantaged child cannot hope to lead a fully satisfying life until he develops a personal security. The horticultural program should include challenging, action-oriented experiences that serve as constructive learning experiences both personally and socially.

The program of activities should help the individual become oriented to his environment and become familiar with its elements. In general, they will gain an understanding when concepts are developed through their own experiences with concrete learning materials and participation on a real and physical level. A program that stresses survival (growing food) can motivate the individual on a level whereby he gets "turned on" to himself and to his own development. It puts him in touch with basic needs and feelings. By experiencing his own success, he can become aware of his strengths and potentials. Seeing change and growth can provide a way to view himself in a more realistic and functional perspective.

When planning an activity, try to relate it to the culture and to the real world of the disadvantaged. Things familiar to us may not be familiar to them, and it is necessary to interpret and translate ideas and concepts through other cultural contexts that are familiar and understandable. For example, a study of the peanut and the sweet potato can be related to the life of George Washington Carver. If it is a study of seeds, introduce concepts by discussing seeds as food. Planning a school or a community garden introduces the participants to new learning experiences and skills. They read cultural directions, deal with experiences in measurements and time, and become familiar with the names of seeds, vegetables, flowers, and garden tools. There are many horticultural activities that will help them refine their manual skills, provide practice in reading, and offer satisfaction by finishing a project.

Community Gardening for the Disadvantaged

The Senate of the United States recently passed the following resolution: "that each American family be urged, where possible, to plant a vegetable garden for the purpose of fighting inflation, saving money, getting exercise, and having the fun and pleasure of family vegetable growing."

The concept of a community garden is not new. It began in Colonial times, and it was very important in the United States during World War II as the "victory garden." Community gardens are very popular in Europe. In Germany, they are called "Kleingarten" (small gardens); in Denmark and Sweden, "Kolinhave" (colony gardens); in Holland, "Volkstumen" (family gardens); and in England, "allotments."

In recent years, several American communities have organized gardens to provide people with garden plots, usually 12 by

15 feet, 15 by 20 feet, or 25 by 30 feet, at a nominal rental fee. At Ann Arbor, Michigan, the Huron Valley National Bank and the University of Michigan cosponsored a 2,000-family community garden project. The YMCA of Asheville, North Carolina began a community garden project for persons living in an integrated apartment complex. In this program, both blacks and whites participated together, and racial differences were nonexistent in the garden environment. Gardening helps to sustain the spirit, and it teaches vital lessons about living in peace with the earth. Urbanites can literally turn over a new leaf by putting down roots within their own community!

Community gardens may be located in urban, suburban, and in rural areas. Many are sponsored by local organizations and agencies. The National Garden Bureau and the Men's Garden Clubs of America have been very instrumental in encouraging more communities to organize such gardens. Churches and private companies have sponsored many community gardens on their unused land. The newest upsurge in community gardening is corporate participation. This is reminiscent of nineteenth century "paternalism" when factory owners built entire communities for their employees. Contemporary companies are now offering fringe benefits that extend to a piece of fertile, company earth. Employees utilize their lunch hour, come to work a little early, leave a little later, or spend their weekends attending their private garden plots. Public housing developments and neighborhood citizens groups have organized gardens on inner city lots helping to promote better community relations in neighborhoods of mixed racial and ethnic backgrounds. On the rural scene, the Frank P. Graham Experimental Farm and Training Center in Anson County, North Carolina, offers a free training program to disadvantaged rural people who wish to learn natural farming methods to enable them to stay on the land and to urbanites who wish to return to the land. The use of public land in city parks and around schools, museums, and hospitals offers other possible sites to organize a community garden.

Additional information concerning the organization of a community garden can be obtained from "Gardens For All,

Inc.," Shelburne Farms, Shelburne, Vermont, 05482 a nonprofit educational and counseling organization dedicated to the concept of community gardening.

"Let a man learn that everything in nature goes by law, and not by luck, and that what he sows, he reaps."
— Ralph Waldo Emerson

References

Brown, I. C. 1963. *Understanding Other Cultures.* Prentice-Hall, Inc., Englewood Cliffs, N. J.

Chernow, F. B. and C. Chernow. 1973. *Teaching the Culturally Disadvantaged Child.* Parker Publ. Co., Inc., West Nyack, N. Y.

Clyne, P. 1972. *Disadvantaged Adult: Educational and Social Needs of Minority Groups.* Longman Inc., New York

Crow, L. D., W. I. Murray, and H. H. Smythe. 1966. *Educating the Culturally Disadvantaged Child.* David McKay Co., Inc., New York

Frost, J. L. and G. R. Hawkes. 1970. *Disadvantaged Child: Issues and Innovations.* Houghton Mifflin Co., Boston, M.

Henson, K. T. 1973. "Who are the disadvantaged?" *Clearing House* 48: 117-120

Riessman, F. 1962. *The Culturally Deprived Child.* Harper and Row, New York

Tiedt, S. W. (ed.). 1968. *Teaching the Disadvantaged Child.* Oxford Univ. Press, New York

Chapter Five

THE FUNDAMENTAL FACTORS
FOR PLANT GROWTH

IT is imperative that one understand the factors necessary for plant growth. These include light, temperature, water, essential elements, and growing media.

GROWING MEDIA

The growing medium is the immediate physical environment of plants. It provides physical support for the roots, and through it the plant receives water, nutrients, and oxygen. The growing medium must be in good condition, and it must meet certain standards. It may be in the form of soil, or it may be a soilless mixture.

Soil

Soil is basically an accumulation of particles which have resulted from the action of weather on rocks. These "dirt" particles alone will not support plant growth. Other components are necessary: organic matter, living organisms, air moisture, and nutrients.

There are three basic soil types:

Clay is a heavy soil composed of very small particles that fit together tightly often resulting in runoff of water. Once water is absorbed, aeration is limited, and when a clay soil dries, it is impermeable to water or air.

Sand is a lighter soil of larger particles, but water drains too rapidly and nutrients are leached out.

Loam is the ideal soil containing a balance of different sizes of particles as well as humus. The granular structure allows for proper drainage and free air circulation, and roots can grow easily. Average loam has about one-half silt, one-quarter clay, and one-quarter sand.

Soil can be considered from two viewpoints, indoors and outdoors. The understanding of these viewpoints is important especially in indoor gardening because here the requirements for plant growth are limited, whereas in outdoor gardening nature can provide at least the minimum requirements.

Outdoors

A well-drained soil is necessary. This is one in which the water moves through quickly so that there is always movement of air through the soil. When water completely replaces the air in the soil, the roots suffocate. Roots will not develop without a constant supply of oxygen and a constant removal of carbon dioxide.

The ideal soil for flowers and vegetables is a rich, sandy loam. One way to change a heavy clay soil or a light sandy soil to a rich loam is by adding organic matter such as compost, peat moss, manure, sawdust, or ground bark. These help to open up tight clay soils, improve drainage, and allow air to move more freely through the soil. In sandy soils, organic matter helps to hold moisture and nutrients. The quantity of organic matter must be large enough so that at least one third of the final mix is organic matter. Spread a layer of organic matter over the soil at least two inches thick and work it in to a depth of four inches. Spread the normal amount of inorganic fertilizer over the organic material (3-4 pounds of 5-10-5 per 100 sq. ft.) and mix thoroughly. If you use peat moss, add ground limestone at the rate of 5 pounds per 100 square feet. If you add raw sawdust, the amount of fertilizer will have to be increased to compensate for the action of the bacteria that work on the sawdust. Without additional nitrogen, the bacteria rob the soil of nitrogen while breaking down the sawdust. For every ten cubic feet of sawdust, add one-half pound of nitrogen.

Before preparing the garden plot, check the pH. The soil pH is very important because it controls the availability of nutrients in the soil. A pH of 7.0 indicates a neutral soil, a lower number indicates acidity, and a higher number indicates alkalinity. A pH of 5.5 to 6.5 is suitable for most plants.

The soil should not be worked while it is wet. The usual test is to squeeze together a handful of soil. If it sticks together in a ball and does not readily crumble, it is too wet to work. Samples should also be taken a few inches below the surface. Soil that sticks to tools is too wet.

The soil should be worked into a suitable seedbed that is not course or lumpy, but free of stones. Strive for a granular rather than a powdery-fine condition.

Indoor Soil Mixes

There are many "recipes" for soil mixes, yet there is no one mixture for all plants. A suitable mix is one-third top soil, one-third sand, and one-third leaf compost or peat moss. It is not wise to use soil from outdoors for indoor gardening unless it has been pasteurized and conditioned. If you use outdoor soil, collect it from a long-established pasture that has not been treated with herbicides. To pasteurize soil, place it in a shallow baking pan and add one cup of water for each gallon of soil. Heat it in an oven at 180 degrees F for 45 minutes and cool for 24 hours before using.

It is also wise to avoid packaged potting soils that are offered in many stores. Some are inferior and adulterated with muck to look very black and rich. Many lack granular consistency, are too dense and heavy, and tend to compact after being watered. If you must use prepackaged soil, check the ingredients. To condition the soil, use peat moss, perlite, vermiculite, or sand. Peat moss increases the organic content, helps to prevent soil from packing into a hard mass around the roots, retains moisture, and prevents the soil from drying out. Perlite is a white, volcanic substance that keeps the soil porous. Vermiculite is expanded mica that soaks up water and retains moisture in the soil. Sand helps to loosen the soil so that air and water can circulate freely.

Indoor Soilless or Synthetic Mixes

The new soilless mixtures such as "Jiffy Mix®," "Redi-

Earth®," "Pro-Mix®," "First Step®," "Super-Soil®," and the Cornell peatlike mixes offer many advantages for indoor gardening: (1) they are uniform; (2) they are light in weight; (3) they are free of weeds and disease organisms; (4) they are easy to obtain; and (5) they are easy to store. Some disadvantages are: (1) the mixture is so light that plants tend to become top heavy; (2) a regular fertilizing program must be maintained; and (3) there is a buildup of insoluble salts. However, these disadvantages can be eliminated by using more drainage material on the bottom of the container, by considering all-purpose and slow-releasing fertilizers, and by slushing the medium with plain water from time to time.

The following are some "recipes" for synthetic mixes:

Cornell Foliage Plant Mix (1 bushel)

Sphagnum peat moss (screened 1/2 inch mesh)	1/2 bushel
Horticultural vermiculite (No. 2)	1/4 bushel
Perlite (medium grade)	1/4 bushel
Ground dolomite limestone	8 tablespoons
20% superphosphate (powdered)	2 tablespoons
14-7-7 Peter's® slow-release fertilizer	3 tablespoons
Granular wetting agent (Aqua-Gro®)	3 tablespoons

This mix is recommended for such plants as Hedera, Amaryllis, Begonias, Caladiums, Citrus, *Coleus,* Ferns, Pelargoniums, Marantas, Palms, Pileas, and *Tradescantia.*

Cornell Epiphytic Mix (1 bushel)

Sphagnum peat moss (screened 1/2 inch mesh)	1/3 bushel
Douglas, red or white fir bark	1/3 bushel
Perlite (medium grade)	1/3 bushel
Ground dolomite limestone	8 tablespoons
20% superphosphate (powdered)	6 tablespoons
14-7-7 Peter's slow release fertilizer	3 tablespoons
Granular wetting agent (Aqua-Gro)	3 tablespoons

This mix is recommended for the following plants and others that can withstand drying out between waterings: African violets, Aloes, Bromeliads, Cacti, Crassula, Episcias, Gloxinias, Hoyas, Philodendrons, Dieffenbachias, Pothos, Peperomias.

Other mixes
1 part sphagnum peat moss
1 part horticultural vermiculite
1 part perlite (medium)
1 tablespoon ground limestone or dolomitic lime for each
7 quarts, or 1/2 to 1 cup of crushed egg shells per quart.

Use this mix for tropical plants which require good drainage and aeration, and can withstand drying out between waterings. Plants having coarse, tuberous, or rhizomatous roots are in this category. The mix is satisfactory for Gesneriads, Bromeliads, Hoyas, Dieffenbachias, Philodendrons, and Peperomias.

3 parts sphagnum moss   2 parts sphagnum peat moss
2 parts hort. vermiculite   1 part hort. vermiculite
                   OR
2 parts perlite (medium)   1 part perlite (medium)
1 tbsp. Lime per 7 qts.   1 tbsp. lime per 7 qts.

This mix is heavier and retains moisture longer. It is used for plants with fine root systems such as African violets, Ferns, Oxalis, Begonias, Caladiums, Citrus, *Coleus*, Marantas, Pileas, and Ficus.

A mixture that is satisfactory for cacti and succulents is the following:

1 part sphagnum peat moss
2 parts horticultural vermiculite
2 parts perlite (medium)
1 tbsp. of lime per 7 qts. of mix

This mix provides for good drainage and low moisture retention.

WATER

Water is essential to plant life. Plant tissue consists of from 60 to 90 percent water. In order for the roots to absorb their food it must be in a very weak solution, and it must still be in a liquid form to circulate through the plant. Water must be available so that the plants can take it up easily. It must be stored in the tiny spaces between the soil particles. Too much water is as undesirable as too little. An excess of water drives out the oxygen that the roots must obtain, and too much water washes away valuable nutrients. Excess water also interferes with nitrification and other processes of soil microorganisms.

Factors that influence the frequency of watering are moisture in the air (humidity), the season, the temperature, light, the container, and the planting medium.

Container and Indoor Plants

Basic guidelines for watering indoor plants and plants in containers are listed below:

1. Overwatering causes root injury and death of plants. Learn to water when the plant needs it. Feel the soil. More plants die of overwatering than from any other factor.
2. A cool environment requires less water than a hot, dry one.
3. When a plant is growing new leaves or producing flowers, it needs more water.
4. Plants with heavy, thorny, or waxy leaves need less water than the thin-leaved varieties. Water cacti once ever 2 to 4 weeks in the summer, and once every 2 months in winter.
5. Wet the soil until the excess water drains off.
6. Water less with plastic pots, more with clay pots.
7. Small pots dry out faster, as do hanging plants.
8. If the plant is rootbound, it will need more water than when just starting to fill the pot with roots.
9. Newly transplanted seedlings or repotted plants need less water until the roots get established, but do not let the seedlings dry out.
10. Water "sick" plants sparingly. The roots are weak and they are likely to rot.
11. Water with tepid water; cold water can shock and cause leaf damage.
12. Water from the tap may contain chlorine and it should stand overnight before being used. Avoid water that is softened with chemicals. Use rain water or cover the surface of the soil with charcoal to strain out some of the

chemical impurities.

13. Rain water or soft water is ideal for watering. It is slightly acid, and it favors the growth of soil bacteria which break down organic matter in the soil.

14. Hard or alkaline water contains salts of calcium and magnesium, in addition to chlorides and sulfates. High concentrations of salts may injure the plant's roots and leaves.

15. Dry heat indoors during winter means more frequent watering. With indoor plants, a lack of humidity is detrimental due to excessive evaporation. Increase the humidity by placing a layer of damp pebbles in trays under the pots or by spraying the plants with a fine mist everyday. Do not mist plants such as cacti or succulents, or those with fuzzy leaves.

Outdoor Watering

The frequency of outdoor watering depends on the type of soil, the sun, the wind, and the variety and size of the plants.

1. Do not water late in the day so that leaves stay wet at night; this encourages plant diseases.

2. In most areas, the garden requires an inch of water a week during the growing season.

3. It is better to give the garden a good soaking once a week than to water it sparingly more often. Water thoroughly to a depth of 6 to 10 inches. Good soaking encourages deeper root growth, whereas light watering encourages shallow root development.

4. Water any time of the day without fear of foliage burning, provided the water is free of salt.

5. Avoid too much water, as it leaches out plant nutrients from the soil and suffocates the root system.

6. To determine the correct amount of water in the soil, squeeze a handful of soil. If the soil is too dry, it will crumble when the hand is opened. If the soil is too wet, water can be squeezed out. If the soil forms a ball which crumbles when dropped, the soil has enough water for

plant growth.

ESSENTIAL ELEMENTS

The following elements are necessary for plant growth: nitrogen, phosphorus, potassium, calcium, sulfur, magnesium, iron, copper, zinc, boron, manganese, sodium, aluminum, oxygen, molybdenum, chlorine, carbon, and hydrogen.

Nitrogen is responsible for the color of foliage, and it also promotes the growth of leaves and stems, but too much has a negative effect on flowering. Phosphorus helps in flowering, root growth, and the production of fruits and seeds. Potassium and potash build resistance to disease and help regulate growth and strengthen stems. These elements are constantly being washed away and must be replenished by applying fertilizers.

Fertilizers

The term *fertilizer,* is used to describe any material that provides plants with the essential elements to complete their life cycles. Fertilizers may be organic or inorganic. In general, there is no perfect fertilizer. A weakness of organic fertilizers is that they are not available to the plants in the early spring before the soil warms up. The microorganisms that break down the organic compounds are dormant at 42° F and become active above 60° F. A quickly soluble chemical or inorganic fertilizer is helpful at this time. Later in the season, however, organic fertilizers have the advantage of slower nutrient release, but heavy applications are needed (100 pounds/1000 sq. ft.). Inorganic fertilizers may burn, but so can some organic fertilizers. It is wise to use both organic and inorganic fertilizers. An inorganic fertilizer high in nitrogen will balance a low nitrogen organic source. Some organic fertilizers are listed below:

Bone meal: Steamed bone meal is slow acting, and raw bone meal is even slower. It is rich in phosphorus, but it is in a form that is so unavailable that the plant may never make use of it. Superphosphate is a better choice for phosphorus.

Dried blood: Processed blood contains much nitrogen, and

it lasts longer than chemical fertilizers.

Animal manures: They are not as rich as generally believed, but they are excellent soil conditioners. It must be used in a decomposed state (not raw) so that the plants are not injured by burning.

Fish emulsions: They are rich in nitrogen but smelly.

Seaweed: Seaweed is very high in potassium but low in nitrogen. Trace elements are also present.

Wood ashes: Wood ashes are high in potassium but low in nitrogen.

Guidelines

1. Do not overfeed; too much can burn the roots and stunt the plants.
2. Do not feed plants during dormancy (December and January) or during illness. The roots cannot make use of the fertilizer, and it may injure their roots.
3. Add fertilizer to soil that is moist, never dry.
4. Foliar feeding by spraying the leaves with a weak solution is helpful especially with epiphytes such as orchids.
5. Do not apply fertilizer to annuals until they show three sturdy leaves.
6. Use a slow-release fertilizer on lawns.
7. Use a fast-acting fertilizer on flowers and vegetables.
8. Fast-growing and flowering plants can be fed very dilute solutions once a week; others, twice a month.
9. Potted plants have roots that are confined and use up food quicker.
10. For vegetables, apply one level teaspoon of 5-10-5 per one square foot of soil about three weeks after the plants have reached the two-leaf stage, and again once every three weeks. Mix the fertilizer into the top 1/2 inch of soil and water thoroughly.
11. With soilless mixes, fertilize at the very start. Use 1/10 to 1/8 of the amount called for with each watering. Every two weeks flush the medium with plain water to wash out accumulated salts.

12. Vary the fertilizer from time to time. Use 20-20-20, then, 23-19-13, and so on.
13. There is no perfect fertilizer. Organic fertilizers should be used with another, or with inorganic fertilizers, if a balanced program is to be maintained.
14. Fertilizers alone cannot improve the soil structure, or compensate for poor plants or seeds.
15. To fertilize a vegetable plot, work in the fertilizer during the soil preparation. If 5-10-5 is used, apply 3 pounds per 100 square feet. Use half of this to turn under and the rest to mix into the top three inches. After the crops are growing, feed them by side dressings. Dig a 2-inch furrow on each side of a row. Apply 5-10-5 at the rate of 1 pound per 100 feet of furrow, and then water. It is better to feed in frequent small doses than in one large one.
16. A new vegetable fertilizer developed by O. M. Scott & Sons, called Vegetable Garden Fertilizer® can be used on all vegetables. It is sprinkled on the soil and worked into the upper inch or two. It is slow releasing, and it is also residual. The plants only have to be fed once during the growing season.
17. Time-released fertilizers are helpful, for they act according to temperature and moisture, they do not leach, and they do not burn roots. Osmocote® 18-6-12 feeds plants for 8 months; Agriform® 20-10-5 feeds up to two years; Agriform 14-4-6 feeds 3 to 4 months; Magamp® 7-40-6 feeds all types plants for a year; and Eeesy Grow® is available in packets that feed for one, five, or eight years.
18. In a 100 pound bag of 5-10-5 fertilizer, the first number is for nitrogen, the second for phosphorus, and the third for potassium. There is 5 percent or 5 pounds of nitrogen present, 10 percent or 10 pounds of phosphorus, and 5 percent or 5 pounds of potassium present. The remaining 80 pounds in the bag consists of materials that are necessary to bind these three elements together, and in a form that the plant can use. There may also be trace elements present, but check the label.

LIGHT

Light is one of the most important factors affecting plant growth, and it is a factor over which you have the least control. Light is the source of energy for all plant growth. It is involved in the complex process of photosynthesis. The amount of light or day length is also important for flowering. This is called photoperiodism. Plants are classified into three groups:

1. *Long-day plants*: These flower during the long days of summer (14 hours or more of maximum light). Examples are Dahlias, Delphiniums, and Tuberous Begonias.
2. *Short-day plants*: These require shorter day lengths such as in the fall. Examples are Chrysanthemums, Gardenias, and Poinsettias.
3. *Indifferent*: These are unaffected by day length. Examples are African violets, Carnations, and Roses.

Guidelines

1. Vegetable plants grow better in full sunlight than in the shade, and some need more sun than others.
2. Some indoor plants can stand direct sunlight, but most prefer a relatively strong, filtered, or diffused light.
3. A plant that lives with insufficient light might look well for months, but it is actually suffering. The amount of light that a plant needs is more than most people think.
4. Artificial lighting may be used alone or in combination with natural light.
5. Use the shadow test to determine the amount of light. Hold a piece of paper up to the light and note the shadow it makes. A sharp shadow means that you have bright or good light, whereas a barely visible shadow means dim light.
6. A full sun requirement means that the plant will need sun for at least half of the day. Indirect or partial sun means that the sun should be filtered through a curtain. Bright light means no direct sun, but the room should be bright and well lighted. Shade-loving plants should be kept in a

well-shaded area with no direct sun at all.

7. When plants are not getting enough light, the lower leaves die, and the new leaves are small. When plants get too much light, they wilt, fade, or burn.

8. Rotate plants so that the leaves get an even distribution of light.

TEMPERATURE

Temperature controls growth and is important in conjunction with other factors. Plants can be grouped into three temperature-requiring categories:

Warm: 62-65°F (16-18°C) at night and up to 80-85°F (27-30°C) in the daytime.

Temperate: 50-55°F (10-13°C) at night up to 65-70°F (18-21°C) during the day.

Cool: 40-45°F (5-7°C) at night and 55-60°F (13-15°C) during the day.

Guidelines

1. Temperatures that are comfortable for people are also satisfactory for most indoor plants (55-65°F at night, 70-75°F during the day).

2. Most plants prefer to be 10 to 15 degrees cooler at night.

3. Keep plants away from drafts, air conditioners, and radiators.

4. All plants benefit from proper temperature and a gentle circulation of air.

5. Most plants do not like sudden changes in temperature.

6. Planting outdoors depends on the temperature. You need to know the frost-free date in the spring, and the average date for the first killing frost in the fall. Your local Cooperative Extension Agent can tell you the average frost-free dates in the spring and fall for your locality.

Chapter Six

BASIC HORTICULTURAL TECHNIQUES

PROPAGATION

ONE of the most interesting aspects of growing plants is propagation. Propagation covers the raising of new plants from seeds, divisions, cuttings, layerings, budding and grafting.

Seeds

A seed is a wonderful mystery. Growing a plant from a seed takes patience, but the results can be very satisfying. Two basic factors are essential for seed growth: moisture and warmth. Oxygen and sometimes light are also necessary. For convenience, the planting of seeds can be divided into those that are sown outdoors and those that are started indoors.

Starting Seeds Indoors

In the temperate and colder regions, crops such as tomatoes, peppers, egg plant, early lettuce, early cabbage, and cauliflower must be started indoors or in cold frames. By sowing seeds indoors, one can gain 4 to 6 weeks over those seeds sown directly into beds outdoors. It is also advantageous to sow indoors seeds that are expensive, very fine, or that take a long time to germinate.

Containers

Almost any type of container or receptacle will do for starting seeds. Flats, peat pots, starter pellets, aluminum pie pans, egg and fruit cartons, window-boxes, and milk cartons can be used. Just about any container that will not disintegrate when filled with moist soil can be used. An essential requirement is that they be 2 to 3 inches deep. There must also be proper drainage. Holes can be made in plastic containers with a hot pick, or a layer of drainage material can be used in containers without holes. Cover the trays, pots, and flats with large plastic bags to hold in moisture and warmth. Heating cables under flats can also be used to hasten germination.

Use plastic milk containers cut in half for starting seeds. When planting in milk cartons made of paper, cut off the bottom to remove the plants easily before transplanting. Seeds can also be planted in small plastic bags partially filled with growing media.

Growing Media

The growing medium must be pasteurized to remove any disease organisms. If soil is used, it should consist of one part loam, one part sand, and one part peat moss. Other growing media may be used such as peat moss, sand, vermiculite, or any of the other commercial synthetic mixes. Avoid using perlite alone to start seeds, for it is quite cool and does not absorb much moisture. Vermiculite alone may hold too much water. Milled sphagnum moss may be used alone, but do not let it dry out, for it forms a crust on its surface. Use a mixture of peat moss and sand, especially for cacti and fine seeds. Synthetic mixes are also suitable for most seeds.

Peat pots, trays, and strips are convenient to use. They are filled with media, and the seed is planted directly in them. No transplanting is needed. The plant is set out in the garden in the same container. Pellets, cubes, and blocks of compressed peat can also be used. Jiffy-7 pellets expand when moistened, and the seed is planted directly into them. BR-8 blocks and Kys-Kubes already contain fertilizer.

Guidelines

1. The usual rule is to cover the seeds with soil or media three to four times the diameter of the seed.

2. Fine seeds (Snapdragons, Petunias, Ageratum, Foxglove, Canterbury Bells, Begonias, Portulaca) are not covered with soil but are merely pressed into the medium. Fine seed may be sown with a seed vibrator or with a fine pepper shaker. Some of the smaller seeds can be started in moist cloth until they germinate, and then are transplanted.
3. Seeds with hard or thick coats must be notched or scratched before they will germinate.
4. Some seeds benefit by being soaked overnight in water to speed germination (beans, peas, Nasturtium, sweet peas).
5. Seeds germinate faster at warm temperatures (70-80°F).
6. Moisture is the limiting factor — too little can result in failure, whereas too much can induce rotting and damping off.

Starting Seeds in Flats

1. Cover the bottom of the flat with a sheet of newspaper, and then cover this with drainage material to a depth of ½ to 1 inch.
2. Add the planting medium to about ½ inch from the top of the flat.
3. Firm the medium with a block of wood, and then thoroughly moisten the medium before planting the seeds by spraying it or by immersing the flat up to its rim in a tub or sink. Keep the medium moist, but not soaking wet. Let it drain.
4. Make rows with a piece of lath or a pencil to the specified depth. Plant seeds in rows about 2 inches apart. Fine seeds may be broadcasted over the surface.
5. Cover the seeds with fine, screened soil or media. Press down the surface gently with a flat board.
6. Carefully water the surface by spraying or by immersion. Bottom watering prevents disturbance of the seeds.
7. Cover the flat with a newspaper, plastic, or a pane of glass. A shower cap propped up with stakes can be placed over a flat. Whatever is used, a uniform moisture

must be maintained.

8. Place the flat in a warm place (70-80°F), but not in direct sunlight. It can also be placed under fluorescent or artificial lights.

9. Check for germination, and as soon as the seedlings appear, remove the covering and give full light, but not direct sun. Do not let the seedlings dry out. Thin out the plants from time to time.

10. Transplant the seedlings to another flat or pot when they have two sets of true leaves. Transplanting helps the seedling to harden off before being placed outdoors in the direct sunlight.

11. Transplant the seedlings by lifting them from the medium with a pointed stick, teaspoon, or kitchen fork. The medium should be moist so that some of it is taken up also. "Mudding" the roots by dipping them in a thick mixture of soil and water aids in the formation of feeder roots. Space the seedlings 2 inches apart or into individual containers, and set the plants deep — right up to the first pair of leaves.

12. Do not fertilize the plants until the true leaves are present. The root systems are well developed at this stage, and they can assimilate the fertilizer.

13. Never transplant the seedlings directly into "raw" humus, for this may result in damping off or stem rot.

14. Gradually harden the plants before placing them outdoors by increasing the amount of sunlight, by withholding water, by providing a lower temperature (60-65°F), and by increasing the ventilation around the plants.

15. Thoroughly water the transplants before they are to be set out. Water them every two or three days until they become established. Give them some shade during this time.

Additional Guidelines and Suggestions

1. Some seeds need an after-ripening period before they will

germinate. Some require stratification or alternate freezing and thawing to break dormancy (native annuals, shrubs, trees, perennials, and wild flowers). Some need scarification or a breakdown of their outer seed coat by scratching it or by treating it with acid.

2. Seedlings growing in soilless media must be fed a liquid fertilizer to keep them healthy. Use Rapid Gro®, Miracle-Gro®, Hyponex®, or Plant Marvel® diluted to one-quarter for very small seedlings, increasing the strength to one-half.

3. Damping off can be controlled by using Semesan® Captan®, and Spergone®.

4. Sow seeds that develop at the same rate — do not plant a slow-growing perennial with a fast-growing annual.

6. Many seedlings benefit by having their shoot tips pinched off; this encourages them to branch and to become compact and bushy.

7. To speed germination, use heat in the form of an electric cable under the flats, or make an incubator by placing a 7½ watt bulb inside of an aluminum pot, and then place the container inside of this.

8. To protect newly transplanted seedlings from intense sun, heat, wind, and even frost, make paper cones out of newspapers or wax paper, cut off the tops of these cones, and place them over the plants. An inverted clay pot placed over the plants, or a light covering of straw or grass clipping will also protect them.

9. Some companies sell very fine seed in a coated form to increase its size for easier planting.

10. Seed tapes facilitate the planting of seeds the right distance apart, and also very fine seeds can be spread evenly. Tapes vary from 15 to 40 inches in length, and they are transparent and dissolve readily the first time the seedbed is watered.

Sowing Seeds Outdoors

1. Cultivate the soil to at least a depth of 8 inches. Be sure

that it drains well, and that the surface is granular and
level.

2. Water the bed the day before planting, or water the furrows before planting the seeds to assure germination.

3. Sow the seed according to depth and space requirements.

4. Water again with a fine spray. Keep the soil moist, but not
waterlogged. To retain moisture, peg burlap to the soil,
and water the burlap lightly.

5. After germination, thin the plants when the soil is moist
to prevent wilting. If you wish to transplant the seedlings,
do it when they have 3 to 4 true leaves, and do not let the
roots dry out.

6. Protect new emerged seedlings from frost with hotcaps or
plastic coverings (tops of plastic milk cartons). These also
help to warm the soil and offer protection from drying
winds.

7. Mulch to keep down weeds and to retain soil moisture.

ASEXUAL OR VEGETATIVE REPRODUCTION

New plants can be propagated from divisions, cuttings, layerings, budding and grafting techniques. Some advantages to this
type of propagation are:

1. The cuttings and divisions develop into plants that are
identical to the parent plant.

2. A new plant can be produced in a short time.

3. Pruning plants for cuttings encourages branch formation.

4. It is a simple procedure.

Divisions

Plants that form multiple crowns and shoots can be divided
into two or more plants, each part having a portion of the
original root system and top growth. Some plants separate
themselves, but a cut through the crown of the plant may be
necessary. Do not cut the new clumps too small, and be sure to
include vigorous parts from which new plants will start.

Aspidistra, Asparagus ferns, many perennials, multiple-crowned African violets, *Calathea,* and ferns can be divided easily.

Cuttings

Cuttings may be taken from the stem, branches, leaves, and roots.

Stem and Branch Cuttings

Any plant that has a stem or branches can be propagated through cuttings. Depending on the plant, there are softwood and hardwood cuttings. Some are rooted with ease, and others with difficulty. Hardwood cuttings will take longer to root. They should be cut during the growing period in late spring and summer. Softwood cuttings generally take one to three weeks, and they can be cut any time of the year. Most house plants are in this category. Successful rooting is dependent on constant moisture and warmth. The basic steps are as follows:

1. Select a middle-aged stem or branch. Very young shoots do not have adequate food reserves to produce roots, and older stems may be past the root-producing stage.
2. Cut off a piece about 3 inches long with at least two leaves attached. Cut the stems about ¼ inch below the leaf joint or node. Remove all leaves from the section that will be below the surface of the rooting medium.
3. Use a medium of moist sand, peat moss, perlite, vermiculite or combinations of these. One part perlite mixed with one part peat moss is very satisfactory.
4. Make a hole in the medium, insert the cutting, and firm the medium around it. Do not let any leaves touch the rooting medium or rotting occurs. The rooting process can be speeded up by first dipping the cut end in a rooting powder or hormone such as Rootone® or Hormodin®. Shake off any excess powder, and then insert the cutting into the medium.
5. Mist the cuttings and cover them with a plastic bag. Place the cuttings in a warm, bright place, but not in direct sun.

Bottom heat speeds up the rooting process.

6. Check for roots after a week, and mist if necessary. Transplant the cuttings when the roots are 1 to 2 inches long.

Guidelines and Suggestions

1. Many softwood cuttings can be rooted in a glass jar filled with water. The top of the jar is covered with plastic and secured with a rubber band. Slits are cut in the plastic, and cuttings are slipped through into the water. To support small cuttings that will not stand in water by themselves, cut pieces of Styrofoam, punch holes in them, place the cuttings through the holes, and float them on the water.

2. Mini-propagators can be made from clear plastic shoe or bread boxes, aquariums, plastic bags, or containers covered with plastic. Sticks or stakes can be used to prop up the plastic bags. Do not let any leaves touch the sides of the bag because they will rot. A very simple propagation unit makes use of a clear plastic or polyethylene bag. Wrap a ball of damp sphagnum moss around the base of several cuttings, insert the cuttings into the bag, and tie the top.

3. An apple crate or a similar wooden box can be made into a larger propagation unit. Cut one side down to about 6 inches (this will be the front). Cut the two sides at 45 degree angles to the front. Leave the rear side or back intact. Fill the box with 3 to 4 inches of medium, and cover the top of the box with plastic. A sheet of plastic can be mounted in a frame and fitted with hinges to produce a hatch door.

4. Florist's oasis can be used to root cuttings. Soak the oasis in water, insert the cuttings, and cover with a plastic bag.

5. Cuttings can be placed under fluorescent lights. Set them about three inches from the lights, and keep the temperature at 70-75 degrees F.

6. Stem cuttings of cacti, succulents, geraniums, and Poinsettias should be allowed to dry at least 24 hours before planting. This prevents possible rot.

7. Another propagation set up can be made by plugging the bottom of a small two inch clay pot, and placing it into a larger six inch clay pot containing rooting medium. Fill the small pot with water, and this will keep the medium moist. The entire unit is covered with a plastic bag.

8. A "bedside" propagating unit can be made from a plastic bag stuffed with moist peat moss and with openings slit in the sides of the bag. The cuttings are slipped through the slits into the medium. The cuttings are misted at least once every day.

Leaf Cuttings

The leaves from certain plants can also produce new plants. They are treated the same way as stem cuttings. Cut off the leaf, leaving about 1 inch of petiole (leaf stem). Treat the end of the petiole with a rooting hormone, and insert the petiole in the medium right up to the base of the blade. Firm the medium around the petiole. Tiny new plants will appear at the base of the parent leaf. Do not remove the parent leaf until there is a sizable cluster of plantlets. When these are about a third of the size of the parent leaf, divide the cluster into separate plants. African violets, Gloxinias, Begonias, Peperomias, and various succulents can be propagated in this way.

Plants with large-veined leaves such as Begonias can be propagated by making two or three slashes across the main veins and pinning the leaf to the medium so that the cut edges are in contact with the moist medium. Young plantlets will develop along the cuts, and these can be separated, each with a cluster of roots. Begonias and other plants can also be propagated by *V*-shaped pieces of leaves, each section having a large vein. Insert the point of the *V* into the medium to hold the cutting upright. Small plants develop at the base of the *V*.

To propagate succulents from leaf cuttings, snap or cut off a leaf as close to the main stem as possible. Let the end of the leaf dry for 24 to 48 hours. Place the end of the leaf in a dry medium, and do not cover with plastic. Water only when the leaves appear to shrivel.

Leaf-bud Cuttings

In each leaf axil (where the leaf stem joins the stem), there is a small bud that can produce new growth. Make a cutting so that the leaf and its axillary bud have a section of the stem attached (½ to 1 inch on each side). This is also called a *mallet cutting*. With this method, many more cuttings from a parent plant can be obtained. The sections of stem on either side of the bud furnish food during the prerooting period, and they also support the leaf in the medium. Azaleas, Bougainvilleas, Chrysanthemums, Crotons, Philodendrons, and many ivies can be propagated in this way. A long vine of ivy lacking any leaves can produce new plants by simply coiling the bare vine on moist medium and pinning it down firmly.

Root Cuttings

Cut sections of the larger more fleshy roots into 2- to 3-inch sections. Cut the end of the root nearest the crown of the plant straight across, and the other end on a slant. Insert the cuttings in the medium with the straight cut upward and the slanted end downward. Crowns will develop at the top ends of the cuttings. Plants such as Poppies, *Anemone, Gaillardia*, Phlox, Yucca, and Oriental Poppies can be propagated in this way.

Layering

Layering is a method of propagation in which new plants are formed while still attached to the parent plant. The technique is often used on woody plants that are difficult to propagate by regular cuttings or by seeds.

Air Layering

Single-stemmed plants such as Aralias, Dracaenas, Rubber plants, and Dieffenbachias are propagated best by air layering. Stems that are 1/4 to 3/4 inches in diameter are best. The procedure is as follows:

1. Make a 2-inch upward slit about 1/3 to 1/2 the way through the stem just below some top growth.
2. Dust the inside of the slit with a rooting hormone. Insert a toothpick at the top of the slit to keep it open. Remove any leaves about 3 or 4 inches below and above the slit.
3. Moisten some sphagnum moss, and place it around the slit stem. The stem should also be covered at least 2 inches below the slit. Wrap the moss in plastic, and secure it with rubber bands or Twistems.
4. Make sure that the moss is evenly moist and that it does not dry out.
5. When the moss is filled with roots, cut the stem below the roots and pot up the new plant.

Dieffenbachia can also be propagated by cutting the bare stem into sections, with each section having a node. Place the sections in the medium, either laying horizontally or standing upright. New shoots will form at the nodes.

Branch or Tip Layering

Some plants layer themselves naturally when their lower branches come in contact with the soil. To produce a new plant:

1. Bend an outer branch down to the soil.
2. Remove leaves from the section to be buried, cut a slit 6 to 8 inches back from the tip, and dust the slit with hormone powder.
3. Cover the branch with soil, and fasten it firmly to the ground with a piece of wire.
4. When roots have developed, separate it from the parent plant.

Runners and Stolons

Many house plants **send** out aerial runners which form new plants on their tips. When they come in contact with moist soil, they root, and later they can be separated from the parent plant. The runners can also be twisted on the surface of the soil or extended to a nearby pot and pinned down. Plants such as Strawberry begonias, Spider plants, *Episcia,* and *Ficus repens* can be propagated in this way.

Offsets and Suckers

These are formed at the base of the plant and can be cut off and rooted, or they can be separated from the parent plant after they have developed roots. Succulents, Bromeliads, *Rhoeo,* and many other plants can be propagated in this way.

Propagating Bulbs and Tubers

1. Break off the scales of an Easter lily bulb and plant them.
2. Scales from rhizomatous gesneriads, Achimenes, Kohlerias, and Smithianthas act like seeds, and each produces a new plant.
3. Tubers of tuberous Begonias and Gloxinias can be divided as long as there is at least one eye (growing point) for each division.

Budding and Grafting

Budding and grafting are more complex techniques, and a brief explanation is given under the activity, "Grafting Cacti."

PROPAGATION OF CERTAIN PLANTS

Plant	Method of Propagation
Agave americana Century plant	Division by offsets
Aglaonema Chinese evergreen	Root division, node stem cuttings, or tip cuttings
Aloe	Stem cutting or offsets from base
Anthurium Flamingo flower	Offsets rooted from parent plant
Aphelandra Zebra plant	Stem cuttings of shoot tips

Araucaria	Young growing tips in spring
Norfolk Island Pine	
Asparagus	Root division and seeds
Asparagus ferns	
Aspidistra	Root division
Cast iron plant	
Begonia	
Rex and beefsteak types	Leaf cuttings
Tuberous types	Stem cuttings
fibrous-rooted types	Stem cuttings and seed
Beloperone	Stem cuttings
Shrimp plant	
Bougainvillea	Stem cuttings
Bromelia	Cuttings of lateral shoots
Bromeliads	
Buxus	Stem cuttings
Boxwood	
Cactus	Seeds, offsets, and grafting
Caladium	Root division
Ceropegia	Stem cuttings and bulblets
Rosary vine	
Chlorophytum	From plantlets on flowering stems
Spider plant	
Cissus	Stem cuttings
Grape ivy	
Citrus	Seeds, stem cuttings
Orange, lemon, lime	
Codiaeum	Stem cuttings, air layering
Croton	
Coleus	Seeds and stem cuttings
Crassula argentea	Stem or leaf cuttings
Jade plant	
Cyclamen	Seed
Cyperus	Root division, stem cuttings
Umbrella plant	
Dieffenbachia	Stem cuttings, air layering
Dumb cane	
Dizygotheca	Stem cuttings
False aralia	
	Stem cuttings
Ferns	Root division, spore germination
Ficus elastica	Air layering, tip cuttings
Rubber tree	
Ficus pandurata	Air layering
Fiddle-leaf fig	
Ficus pumila	Stem cuttings
Creeping fig	
Fuchsia	Stem cuttings
Gloxinia	Seeds, leaf cuttings, root division
Gynura	Stem cuttings

Purple passion plant	
Geranium	Seeds, stem cuttings
Hoya	Stem cuttings, layering
Wax plant	
Hedera	Stem cuttings
Ivy	
Impatiens	Seeds, stem cuttings
Kalanchoe	Seeds, leaf cuttings
Maranta	Stem cuttings, root division
Prayer plant	
Mimosa pudica	Seeds
Sensitive plant	
Narcissus	Bulbs
Paper whites	
Orchids	Seeds, division of "pseudo-bulbs"
Oxalis	Seeds, bulbs
Pachysandra	Stem cuttings
Palms	Seed
Peperomia	Leaf and stem cuttings
Pilea cadierei	Stem cuttings
Aluminum plant	
Pilea microphylla	Stem cuttings and seeds
Artillery plant	
Philodendrons	Stem cuttings, mallet leaf cuttings
Plectranthus	Stem cuttings
Swedish ivy	
Podocarpus	Stem cuttings
Pothos	Stem cuttings, mallet leaf cuttings
Rhoeo	Root offsets at base of plant
Moses-in-the-boat	
Saintpaulia	Leaf cuttings, division, seeds
African violet	
Sansevieria	Leaf cuttings, root division
Snake plant	
Saxifraga sarmentosa	Root plantlets from runners
Strawberry begonia	
Schefflera	Stem cuttings
Umbrella plant	
Schlumbergera	Stem cuttings
Christmas cactus	
Senecio	Stem cuttings
German ivy	
Syngonium podophylum	Stem cuttings
Spathiphyllum	Division of rootstock
White flag	
Tolmiea menziesii	Root plantlets arising from
Piggyback plant	leaves
Tradescantia	Stem cuttings
Zebrina	Stem cuttings
Wandering jew	

TRANSPLANTING AND POTTING

Pots

Flower pots and containers are made of clay, plastic, wood, glass, and other rigid materials. They come in all shapes, sizes, and colors. Proper drainage is the most important factor when selecting pots.

Clay pots are porous, allowing excess water and salts to escape and oxygen to enter more easily. Evaporation is greater, however, and plants growing in clay pots must be watered more often. Clay pots are also heavier, but sturdy, and if new, they must be soaked in water to remove any chemicals and to condition the pot so that it will not draw moisture from the soil or growing medium. A clay pot filled with moist soil is 10 to 15 degrees cooler than a plastic pot, which is ideal for root development.

Plastic pots are not porous, and oxygen and water can enter only through the top and bottom of the container. Excess salts cannot escape as readily and may injure the roots. Evaporation is slower in plastic pots, but overwatering could be a problem. Plastic pots are lighter in weight but not as sturdy. It is wise to place more material on the bottom of a plastic pot to increase drainage and to increase its stability. Plastic pots can be cleaned easily, they come in various colors, and large quantities can be stored in a small space.

Peat pots are made from pressed peat. They are light weight, easy to handle, and ideal for transplanting seedlings. A second transplanting is unnecessary, for the roots grow through the sides and the bottom, and some peat pots even contain fertilizer. When a peat pot and its plant is placed in the ground, make sure that it is an inch or so below the soil level. If the peat pot is exposed above the soil, it acts as a wick and the transplant will be dehydrated.

Repotting and Transplanting

A plant is ready for repotting when:

1. The foliage wilts in spite of normal watering.
2. The plant sheds its lower leaves, or they turn yellow and die.
3. The leaves fail to develop to their normal size.
4. The roots protrude out of the drainage hole.

To remove a plant from its pot:

1. Place your hand over the top of the pot, and turn it upside down and gently tap the rim and the sides of the pot against a table with your hand or with a rubber hammer until the root ball falls out.
2. If there is no loose soil, repot the plant. Do not let the root ball dry out during the transplanting process.
3. Place the plant in a pot no more than two inches wider in diameter than the root ball or the original pot (if it was in a 2½-inch pot, put it in a pot no larger than 4 inches; if it was in a 3-inch pot, put it in a 5-inch pot). Overpotted plants can easily become waterlogged.
4. Proper drainage is important. Place pieces of drainage material over the drainage holes to a depth of about ¼ that of the pot. In a holeless container, use at least one inch of drainage material on the bottom. If water accumulates on the bottom, the roots will rot.
5. Place soil or media over the drainage material. Fill the pot three-quarters full, make a slight depression, and press the soil firmly against the sides of the pot.
6. Center the plant in the pot. Add enough growing media until the plant is at the proper height. The top of the root ball should be ½-inch below the rim of the pot for proper maturing and watering.
7. Firm the soil around the root ball and apply pressure to the soil around the rim. Tap the pot on a table or work surface to settle the soil in the pot.
8. Water thoroughly until the water drains through the bottom.
9. A newly potted plant also benefits by being pruned slightly so that the root system can easily supply the top growth with water.

10. If a newly transplanted plant starts to wilt, mist it and cover it with a clear plastic bag until it recuperates from the shock of transplanting. Keep it out of direct sun for a few days.

Suggestions

1. Very large plants do not have to be repotted. Instead remove two inches of soil from the surface, and add new soil. This adds nutrients and removes excess salts.
2. Use bottle caps for drainage material by placing the concave side down over the drainage hole.
3. The summer months are good for repotting plants. During this time, plants are actively growing and can best adapt to the shock.
4. Use clay pots for succulents and cacti. There is less chance for root rot.
5. Make sure that the pots are clean to prevent fungus and other diseases. Scrub the pots with a wire brush to remove any algae and excess salts. Soak the pots in a mild solution of bleach to sterilize them. It is also wise to use clean drainage material.

PINCHING

This practice is used to produce more compact growth. When branches start to grow, they can be induced to produce additional side branches by removing the tips of the growing shoots. This stimulates the lateral buds, which would otherwise remain dormant, to grow. The practice of pinching flower buds also encourages more foliage and larger inflorescences in some plants. Pinch the tips just above a leaf node, and try not to leave a stump.

PRUNING

This practice helps to maintain plants at a reasonable size. It also promotes flower shoots, and it improves the shape of the plant. With a sharp knife, scissors, or pruning shears, make a cut just above the point where a future branch is desired, making sure a bud is present to develop into a new shoot.

Root pruning is practiced to keep large plants in the same container, and to create bonsai. It is done after a good watering, and usually one third of the side roots are removed. The root mass is shaped to fit the pot. It is also wise to prune some of the foliage at the same time. Place the plant in a plastic bag, and keep it out of direct sunlight for a few days.

MULCHING

The advantages to mulching are: (1) it reduces weeding; (2) it reduces watering; (3) it reduces cultivating; (4) it minimizes erosion; (5) it reduces disease control; (6) there is less damage to fruit and leaves from water splashing up; (7) it helps to add nutrients and to condition the soil; and (8) it helps to protect plants during the winter.

Types of mulches include bark chips, buckwheat hulls, cocoa bean hulls, coffee grounds, corn cobs, fiberglass insulation, grass clippings, hay, leaves, peanut and pecan shells, peat, pine needles, polyethylene film (black), sawdust, seaweed, stones and pebbles, straw, sugar cane, and wood chips. Various combinations of the above can be used.

Use 2 to 4 inches of organic mulches to prevent weeds and to retain moisture. The organic mulches will decompose, and they must be replaced. If plastic is used, leave some space around the plants so that water can enter the soil.

TROUBLESHOOTING AND PEST CONTROL

The best defense against pests is good plant hygiene. The surface of the soil should be checked from time to time for fungus, mildew, or other organisms. The leaves should be washed once a month. One method is to dip the foliage in a solution of warm water and mild soap flakes, and then rinse thoroughly.

Overwatering, overfeeding, and neglect cause more plant

deaths than insects do. The first consideration is proper identification of the pest or trouble. It is best to quarantine the plant
and then treat it.

The following charts may help in identifying and treating
diseased or damaged plants.

Symptom	Cause	Treatment
Leaves are pale green, new leaves are small and growth stops, lower leaves turn yellow and drop	not enough fertilizer	Fertilize, especially during active growth
Edges of leaves are dry, brown, and curl under	not enough water or too much heat	Water plant thoroughly and move to a cooler place
Leaves turn yellow and fall off suddenly	a rise or fall in temperature	Place plant away from drafts and heaters
Growth is rapid, but appears weak, and plant wilts often	too much fertilizer	Fertilize less frequently or cut the strength in half, flush the soil with plain water to remove excess salts
Lower leaves turn yellow, stem becomes dark and soft	too much water	Water only when necessary, repot the plant, and provide proper drainage
Edges of leaves turn brown, curl, and fall off	too little humidity	Mist the plant or place it on a tray of moist pebbles, place it in a plastic bag for a few days
Plant is spindly and weak, foliage is pale	too little light	Expose the plant to increased light
Leaves have yellow or brown areas on the upper surface	too much light	Expose the plant to less light, and shield it from direct sun
Plant often wilts, produces small leaves, roots protrude through the drainage holes	plant is root bound	Repot the plant

| No flowers, but lush foliage | too much fertilizer especially nitrogen | Withhold feeding, especially during the winter months, let the soil dry for a short time, and change the light exposure |

————

Pest	Description	Control
Aphids or plant lice	Small (⅛ in.), green, red, yellow, brown, or black insects that suck out plant sap from soft growing shoots, flower buds, and leaves. Growth is stunted and leaves die.	Immerse the plant in a dilute soap solution and rinse in water. If serious, use rotenone, pyrethrum, or malathion. Follow the directions carefully.
Fungus gnats	Small, black, flying insects that lay their eggs on the soil; the larvae feed on the roots.	Drench the soil with lime water or with a nicotine solution.
Mealy bugs	Soft, white, cottony-looking insects that cluster under leaves and in crevices of buds. They suck sap and stunt and eventually kill the plant	Wash with alcohol or immerse in a soapy solution and rinse; if serious, use malathion.
Scale insects	Oval, white, brown, green, or black blisterlike spots on the undersides of leaves and stems; plants turn yellow and die.	Brush off scales with a brush, and immerse in a soap solution; if serious, use rotenone, pyrethrum, or malathion.
Spider mites	Red or green pests that spin fine webs covering the plant; leaves have yellow or brown spots; stunts and eventually kills the plant.	Immerse in a soap solution; if serious, use difocol, tetradifon, malathion.
White flies	Tiny, white flying insects whose larvae feed on sap and eventually kill the plant.	Spray the underside of the leaves with water or with a soap solution; if serious, use rotenone, pyrethrum, or malathion.

Some Plant Diseases

Damp-off: This is the most common of the fungus diseases usually attacking seedlings. It becomes evident when healthy plants suddenly rot off at the soil line. Use pasteurized media or drench the medium with a fungicide such as Pano-Drench®.

Leaf-spot: Symptoms are purple, brown, or black spots on the foliage. The fungal spores are spread by splashing water on the foliage. Spray or dust with ferbame (Fermate®). Infected foliage and blossoms should be removed and burned.

Mildew: Powdery white areas on leaves and stems. Dust with sulfur and provide proper ventilation.

Rot: Attacks stem and roots below the surface of the soil. Soil drenches prevent the fungus from spreading to other plants, but those already infected must be destroyed.

Rust: Blisterlike areas which release rusty-looking spores that spread to foliage by air currents and water. A dusting with Fermate prevents development of the spores.

Virus diseases: Symptoms are light-colored rings of dead cells on the leaves, and also deformed growth. The only treatment is to destroy the infected plant immediately, and try to prevent other plants from becoming infected by sterilizing anything that has come in contact with the infected plant.

Pest Control

Investigate the various insecticides, miticides, fungicides, and general pesticides before you start your gardening program. Safer pesticides are being developed, but more and more reliance is being placed on biological, mechanical, and cultural methods of control. If you *must* use chemical pesticides, make a careful selection, and follow the directions. Many of the non-chemical methods, however, are more adaptable to indoor gardening, and also to outdoor gardening on a small scale.

Chemical Pesticides

Malathion, cythion, carbaryl (Sevin®), diazinon (Spectracide®), and nicotine sulfate (Black leaf 40®) are used against flower, vegetable, lawn, and woody plant pests. These have some degree of toxicity to man, and the directions must be followed carefully. Commercial insecticides that offer a high degree of safety include the dormant oil sprays for scale, white-fly, mites, mealy bugs, leaf rollers, and others. Also, the plant derivatives such as rotenone, pyrethrums, and ryania (Ryatox®) are effective against many chewing and sucking insects. Another safe product is the household cleaner Basic H®, made from soybeans and used for thrips, aphids, and red spider mites. The biological insecticide *Bacillus thuringiensis* (Dipel®, Bio-trol®, Thuricide®) is effective against worm and caterpillar pests. Mesurol (Slug-Geta®) and Snail Snare® are effective against snails and slugs.

Fungicides

Benomyl (Benlate®), Captan, ferbam (Fermate), folpet (Phal-tan®), karathane (Mildex®), maneb (Manzate®, Dithane M-22®), sulfur, and zineb. For mildew, use Acti-Dione PM®, Consan No. 20®, or parinol (Parnon®).

Herbicides

Betasan®, Casoran®, Cloro-IPC®, Dacthal® and Trifluralin®, and Eptam®. Less selective and requiring very careful use are aminotiazole, diuron, monuron, silvex, 2,4-D, and sima-zine.

Some Nonchemical Pesticides

1. Purdue University reports that a spray of 5 pounds of wheat flour and one pint of buttermilk in 25 gallons of water destroys spider mites by immobilizing them on the foliage.
2. Tomato stems and leaves boiled in water and sprayed on plants destroy aphids and other pests. It also acts as a repellent.
3. A solution of water and lime painted on trees deters borers.

4. Lime mixed with wood ashes sprinkled around onions, cabbage, and beets prevents damage by maggots, and also kills squash bugs.
5. Grind up hot peppers, green onions, garlic, mint, geranium leaves, and other strong flavored plants, and make a spray; the more the ingredients, the more insects it is likely to repel.
6. Wood ashes spread on the ground or foliage deter cutworms, bean beetles, squash bugs, borers, slugs and snails.
7. Nematodes are killed by asparagus juice.
8. Garlic is one of the most potent insect repellents.

Mechanical Methods

(1) Hand pick the insects; (2) cover the plants with nets; (3) band tree trunks, and place metal or paper collars around seedlings; (4) aluminum foil mulch repels aphids, thrips, and Mexican bean beetles.

Cultural Controls

1. Choose disease and insect-resistant varieties.
2. Remove weeds that may serve as hosts to pests.
3. Remove decaying plant refuse that may lead to infestations.
4. Remove insect egg cases, except for the foamy cases of the praying mantis.
5. Crop rotation prevents nematode infestations.
6. Till the garden early in the spring to expose insect and slug eggs.

Biological Controls

1. Encourage birds to visit the garden; also, snakes, lizards, and toads.
2. Ladybugs, Trichogramma wasps, and praying mantises are beneficial in the garden.
3. *Bacillus thuringiensis* (Dipel, Biotrol, Thuricide) is used

against the larvae of lepidopterous insects.

4. Entocons are insect hormones (pheromones) that control mealy bugs, scale aphids, and other pests.

Companion Planting

Some plants help others when grown nearby either by repelling insects, acting as a trap crop, or by stimulating growth. The reasoning behind companion planting says Professor R. B. Root of Cornell University is that "the more varied a garden's planting, the less likely the pest damage because the confusion of various chemical stimuli offer by a mixture of plants causes the breakdown of an insect's orientation, feeding habits, and population numbers." The following are some examples:

1. Garlic repels aphids, Japanese beetles, and others.
2. Mint, sage, and mustard protect members of the cabbage family.
3. Savory, cosmos and asters repel bean beetles.
4. Basil protects tomatoes.
5. The Connecticut Agricultural Experiment Station in New Haven has shown that marigolds produce a chemical which kills nematodes.

Chapter Seven

ACTIVITY SECTION

THE following activities are those that can be used in horticultural programs for the disabled and disadvantaged. Each activity was chosen on the basis of its therapeutic benefits with many of the projects having similar therapeutic goals in mind.

The activities cover a wide range of tasks, interactions, and experiences. They include both individual and group projects. Some are creative activities while others are passive and simply provide for relaxation. Be aware that passive activities that involve simply observing nature may be just as therapeutic as those that involve active participation. Some of the activities are intended to stimulate interest and are just for fun and to make use of leisure time. Some are everyday routine tasks, but they are very therapeutic. These include watering plants, washing pots, weeding, thinning, transplanting, staking, harvesting, screening soil, mixing soil, sowing seeds, making cuttings, cleaning foliage, removing dead leaves and plants, and fertilizing. Others have educational and rehabilitative values which may be useful in programs that are designed to train people.

Each activity is coded for its appropriateness for a particular group. A description of the activity is given with various guidelines and suggested projects. These may be modified and adapted to various levels of performance. The diversity of plants that can be grown, the varied work skills needed, and the specific objectives in mind provide the opportunity for great diversification.

Program Code for Activities

The vast majority of the disabled and disadvantaged fall into one or more of the following six groups. These groupings are intended only for programming purposes and should serve only as a guide for those who are planning a horticultural program for a particular group and need to know appropriate activities.

A: Aged — need more sedentary activities that have continuity and that sustain interest

C: Children — need short-term activities that are both interesting and educational

D: Disadvantaged — need challenging, educational, and action-oriented activities

G: General Restriction — need activities that are not too strenuous

MR: Mentally Retarded — need simplified but challenging activities that are programmed for mental capabilities more than physical

NP: Neuropsychiatric — need activities that are planned for social adjustment

A Coded List of Activities

Bonsai — A,D,G,NP
Children's Activities — C,D,MR,NP
Collecting Plant Materials — A,C,D,G,MR,NP
Dish Gardening — A,C,D,G,MR,NP
Drying Plants and Flowers — A,C,D,G,MR,NP
Ecology Boxes — A,D,G,MR,NP
Flower Arranging — A,D,G,MR,NP
Flower Gardening — A,C,D,G,MR,NP
Forcing Bulbs — A,C,D,G,MR,NP
Forcing Flowering Branches — A,C,D,G,MR,NP
Gardening in Containers — A,C,D,G,MR,NP
Gardening in Raised Beds — A,C,D,G,MR,NP
Gardening under Lights — A,C,D,G,MR,NP
Gardens for the Blind — A,C,D,G,MR,NP
Grafting cacti — D,NP
Growing Herbs — A,D,G,MR,NP
Hanging Baskets — A,D,G,MR,NP
Hydroponic Gardening — A,D,G,MR,NP

Kitchen Gardening — A,C,D,G,MR,NP
Sand Painting — C,D,G,MR,NP
Terrariums — A,C,D,G,MR,NP
Topiary — A,D,G,MR,NP
Vegetable Gardening — A,C,D,G,MR,NP
Window Box Gardening — A,D,G,MR,NP
Winter Greens — A,C,D,G,MR,NP

BONSAI

This activity provides the opportunity to blend art and horticulture. It is a process of pruning, shaping, and literally dwarfing a plant to produce a work of art. True bonsai requires a great deal of patience and time. For the disabled, "instant" bonsai is more appealing. The activity may be modified for quick results by selecting plants already stunted, bent, or gnarled, and that can be shaped easily. For "instant" bonsai, more tender and semihardy plants can be used, especially those plants that are naturally dwarf or slow growing, and that have flowers, fruits, and leaves. Select plants with an interesting shape, exposed roots, tapering trunks and branches, and short internodes.

Suggested Plants

Acacia, andromeda, arborvitae, azalea, beech, birch, boxwood, carissa, cherry (flowering), citrus, elm (Chinese), fir, gardenia, hawthorns, holly (Japanese), ironwood, ivy, juniper, maple (Japanese), mimosa, mistletoe fig, myrtle, olive, pine, podocarpus, pomegranate, quince (flowering), roses (miniature), rosemary, serrisa, spruce, yew

Equipment

Various containers, soil, gravel, accessory decorations, pruning shears, trowel, wire cutters, copper wire of various lengths, scissors, tweezers

Containers

Size, shape, color, and depth should complement the plant. All containers should have drainage holes. Gravel should be used over the drainage holes, and an all-purpose soil mixture is satisfactory. Any shallow container can be used, but there are special bonsai containers on the market.

Accessory Decorations

Use moss, stones, and driftwood to decorate the scene.

Training and Shaping

The styles of bonsai include formal upright, informal upright (slanting trunk), slanting, or semicascade, and cascade. These are based on the shape of the plant and how much the main stem slants away from an imaginary vertical axis. To train and shape the plant, proceed as follows:

1. Observe the trunk line to determine the appropriate style. Make a sketch on paper or observe various pictures of completed bonsai as a guide.
2. Next, consider the branches. Look for horizontal branches in threes (one on each side and one in back) at various levels. Prune unnecessary branches and cut branches shorter on one side to imitate the effect of winds.
3. Trim and prune groups of leaves at the top and middle sections, so that groups of foliage resemble clouds. Continuous trimming of new growth results in short, tiny branches.
4. Before potting, it is necessary to prune the roots by cutting them back about one-third. To secure the plant in the pot, pass a piece of wire through the root ball and drainage holes, and twist ends together under the pot.
5. Water the plant thoroughly, and keep it in the shade for a few days. Water frequently and fertilize every three to four weeks with 20-20-20 (half-strength) or fish emulsion.

6. For long-term projects, the branches and trunk are wired by twisting 18-gauge wire around "green" wood that can be bent easily. Do not water the plant the day before wiring so that the branches will be more flexible. Do not wire too tightly, and keep the turns about 1/4 inch apart. The wire must be removed after a growing season, and the plant is given a short rest. Subsequent series of wirings are applied from season to season. The plant is repotted every three to four years with additional pruning of top growth and roots.

Suggest Projects

Boxwood (*Buxus* sp.) is ideal for instant bonsai because of its branching trunk, multiple branches, and small leaves.

Small leaved ivies can be used and are easily trained.

Small pomegranate seedlings in appropriate trays are attractive. Freeze the seeds before sowing them in the spring.

Consider combining boxwood, juniper, and privet in a cement foundation block.

References

Larkin, H. J. 1969. *Bonsai for Beginners.* Arcox Publ. Co., Inc., N.Y.
Nakamura, Z. 1973. *Quick and Easy Bonsai Miniatures.* Japan Pubns., Trading Center, San Francisco
Sunset Editors. 1965. *Bonsai.* Lane Pub. Co., Menlo Park, Ca.
Walker, L. 1975. *Bonsai.* Drake Pubs. Inc., N.Y.

CHILDREN'S GARDENING ACTIVITIES

The following activities and projects are for fun and for learning. Emphasize personal satisfaction and creativity plus the joy of doing, rather than perfection in the finished product. Try to alternate indoor and outdoor activities to sustain interest. Select activities that are within the range of a child's ability and skills, and modify the activities according to individual differences.

Suggested Activities

Plant seeds in peat pellets. The pellets expand from 1/4 inch to 2 inches when watered. They fascinate children.

Make bark, stump, and leaf rubbings. Place a mushroom top on a piece of paper to make spore prints, and then spray with acrylic.

Seed tapes are fun. Plant these in various designs.

Teach children how to make compost in a large plastic bag. Add starter soil, compost material, one cup of agricultural lime, and one cup of water. Turn the bag upside down now and then.

Graft cacti with older children.

Plant a mini-garden (10 feet x 10 feet) with a theme. It may be an herb garden or a Mediterranean garden with tomatoes, eggplant, peppers, onions, and various squashes. It may be a Chinese garden with cabbage, snowpeas, leeks, radishes, cucumbers, and celery.

Make mini-arrangements of dried plant materials in acorn cups, walnut shells, and in small bottle caps.

Take a field trip to a museum, an arboretum, a garden-nursery, or to a flower show.

Make Easter eggs by blowing out the contents of an egg. Decorate the eggs with pressed flowers, ferns, or leaves. Spray with acrylic. Suspend the eggs from the branches of a tree or shrub.

To make a Thanksgiving turkey use a pine cone for the body and pipe cleaners for the feet. Add a feather for a tail.

Children love "action" plants such as radishes, lettuce, onion sets, beans, French marigolds, dwarf zinnias, and cosmos.

Make a garden kit for each child. Include seeds, simple tools, and supplies.

Have children train ivy around stakes. Start with three ivy plants in a pot. Arrange the stakes in the shape of a teepee.

During the winter, make winter scenes on sheets of white Styrofoam. Insert evergreen branches for trees, and spray with artificial snow.

Children love to make miniature dish gardens and flower arrangements. The children can collect their own materials. Provide them with tools such as a pair of tweezers, manicure scissors, and an eyedropper. The children can also carve or mold mini-containers from blocks of wax collected from crayons or candles.

Plant a "generosity garden" for birds and other wild animals. Include sunflowers, popcorn, and catnip.

Plant a tree on Arbor Day.

Make a collection of fruit pods and seeds, and mount them on Styrofoam trays.

Use various seeds to make seed mosaics.

Force paper-white Narcissus bulbs. The flowers are very fragrant.

Grow interesting plants such as Sensitive plants and Venus's-flytraps. Also, try avocado pits, coffee, and citrus seeds. Grow a potato plant in a burlap bag.

Dye living flowers such as Queen Anne's lace and white carnations by inserting the stems in florist's tubes filled with water and vegetable coloring.

Gourds, watermelon, squash, and cucumbers can be grown inside of bottles as a novelty. When the fruit is still small, insert it into a bottle while it is still attached to the vine.

Grow various sprouts. Almost any seeds can be sprouted (corn, barley, alfalfa, lentils, mung beans, soybeans, rye, peas, millet, lima beans, sunflowers). Use a wide-mouthed quart jar, bulb pan, or clay saucer. Soak the seeds overnight, then drain and place in the container. Set the container in a warm, dark place, and rinse and drain the seeds at least twice a day. In three to six days, sprouts will start to germinate. When they are 1 to 3 inches long, they are ready to be harvested. Use them in salads and in sandwiches.

Make mini-hanging baskets from carrots, beets, parsnips, and turnips. Remove the leaves from the top end and cut off about 2 inches from the opposite end. Hollow out the center with an apple corer. Be careful not to cut through to the outside. Make three evenly spaced holes around the rim, thread pieces of string or wire through the holes, and then fasten them together so that the top end is hanging upside down. Fill the cavity with water, and soon leaves will start to grow and turn upward to cover the "basket."

To make egg carton gardens fill empty egg shells with soil and plant seeds in them. Use the egg carton as a planter. After the seeds have germinated, transplant the seedlings, shell and all, into a larger pot or into the garden plot. The shell will provide additional nutrients.

Make a mini-terrarium with a quart jar. Lay the jar on its side on a platform or support made from wood.

To make sponge gardens spread seeds of cress, grass, or lettuce on moist sponges.

To make dough planters mix four parts flour, one part salt, and one and one half parts water. Shape the dough into a pot or container. Make designs on the outside and do not forget a drainage hole in the bottom. Bake in a 350° F oven for an hour. After it cools, shellack or varnish the inside and outside.

To make a mini-greenhouse staple or glue 1/2 inch x 1/2 inch strips of wood together to form the shape of a house. Apply transparent plastic or Saran Wrap®. Place the greenhouse on a metal tray filled with moist gravel.

Plant bean seeds between moist blotters or napkins inserted around the inside of a glass jar. Root growth can be observed.

Soak corn leaves in water and then weave them into ropes or baskets.

A collection of seeds is fascinating. Bean seeds come in a variety of sizes and colors. Seeds of various textures are fascinating to the blind.

Soak Indian corn in water and string it to make necklaces.

Plant seeds in the form of a child's initials.

Root-view boxes can be made by planting seeds or cuttings in a box with a glass front to observe the development of roots. Have a "root-race."

Show colored slides and films of flowers and plant life. Consult your local library.

Children enjoy plants that grow quickly. The growth can be measured from day to day. The following plants are quick to germinate and grow fast: castor beans, sunflowers, morning glory, pumpkins, gourds, zinnias, marigolds, cosmos, radishes, wax beans, green beans, and beets.

Children are fascinated with giant-sized plants, and also midget varieties of vegetables. Refer to the Activity Section — Vegetable Gardening for a list of giant and midget varieties.

Air plants (*Kalanchoe pinnata*) are interesting plants to grow and they are easy to propagate. Simply pin a leaf to a curtain, and it will form numerous plantlets along its edges. To obtain new plants, let the plantlets fall into a pot of soil where they will grow into new plants.

A whistle or horn can be made from a squash leaf stem. The hollow leaf stem or petiole becomes solid where it joins the leaf blade. Cut the leaf stem from the vine and cut it again through the solid part near the leaf. Make a slit in the stalk about 1/2 inch up from the solid part. Put the end with the slit in your mouth and blow.

CHILDREN'S VEGETABLE GARDENS

Many children have no idea where food comes from or how vegetables grow. Children are fascinated with the great variety of fruits and vegetables. Many crops are easy to grow, and, of course, the harvest can be eaten.

Guidelines

1. The program should be planned for the entire growing

season. Plan early in the fall so that the garden plot can be tilled before winter. All equipment, tools, and supplies should be obtained well in advance.

2. The gardening experience should be a personal one for each child. The child should be involved both physically and mentally. Each child should have his own plot, seeds, and tools. A garden kit with necessary supplies can be made for each child.

3. The program should involve some classroom instruction concerning the study of plants, planning the garden, how to handle tools, planting seeds, and cultivating the garden.

4. The size of each garden plot will vary depending on the amount of space and on the experience and age of the child. A small plot for young children may be 4 feet by 8 feet. For the disabled, long and narrow plots or a plot with paths that make every plant within arm's reach are suggested. For older and nondisabled children, the plots may be 8 feet by 10 feet or 10 feet by 11 feet.

5. A heterogeneous group of children (age, sex, race, disability) seems to work out the best. The older and more experienced children often help the younger children.

6. Try to involve the parents also. Have a parent's day so that they can observe the program. Children will often grow vegetables that their parents enjoy. The vegetables may also be taken home with instructions concerning their nutritional value and ways to prepare them.

7. Plan a program that emphasizes success, even if you must help it along. The children must experience immediate satisfaction. Do not be a perfectionist! Every degree of success is acceptable.

8. Select varieties of vegetables that are dependable. Plant a variety of different vegetables so that if one fails, the others will disguise the loss. Younger gardeners should follow a prescribed selection. More advanced gardeners may choose additional varieties that interest them. Many of the midget varieties are interesting and are easy to grow. Choose those varieties that provide a continuous

harvest throughout the season as well as early and late maturing types.

9. Let the children experiment and learn by self-corrective methods, but also provide guidance. Each child must be given a certain amount of individual attention. In most cases, the younger children will have to be assisted in their tasks.

10. The program should include both fun and work. Encourage the children to take care of their gardens by placing stakes with their names in each plot. Daily chores can also be communicated by setting up a bulletin board or chalkboard near the gardens.

11. A demonstration garden often helps to inspire children, and it also encourages a sense of competition or meeting a standard. Children learn by comparing their achievements with others.

12. Encourage the planting of flowers by discussing companion planting. For example, plant some Dwarf Marigolds between rows of lettuce. Other activities may be worked into the program such as weed and insect identification and a study of the soil.

13. Have a harvest picnic or a vegetable-growing contest. Encourage the sharing and trading of the produce. The harvest may also be distributed to senior citizens or sold to supermarkets.

References

Anonymous. 1969. "Child gardeners, how to encourage success, discourage dropping-out." *Sunset* 142: 200-201.

———. 1969. "Garden projects and pastimes for children." *Home Gard.* 56: 33-40.

———. 1971. "Indoor planting adventures for children." *Sunset* 146: 164-165.

———. 1971. "Plants for little people." *Bet. Homes & Gard.* 49: 76.

———. 1972. "Gardening at school? It's a kick." *Sunset* 148: 98-101.

Baker, S. S. 1966. *The Indoor and Outdoor Grow-it-Book.* Random House Inc., New York

Brandhorst, K. and N. Miller. (n.d.). *Green Serendipity: A Handbook of Unexpected Horticultural Discoveries.* Holden Arboretum, Mentor, Oh.

Brilmayer, B. 1965. "Gardening is child's play." *Flower Grower* 52: 54-55.

Charles, R. 1969. "Give the kids a garden of their own." *Parent's Mag.* 44: 77.

Creative Editors. 1973. *How to Have Fun with an Indoor Garden.* Creative Ed. Soc. Inc., Mankato, Minn.

———. 1974. *How to Have Fun with a Flower Garden.* Creative Ed. Soc. Inc., Mankato, Minn.

———. 1974. *How to Have Fun with a Vegetable Garden.* Creative Ed. Soc. Inc., Mankato, Minn.

Dole, L. E. 1973. *Herb Magic and Garden Craft.* Sterling Pub. Co., Inc., New York

Doughty, W., R. Hildebrand, C. Malcolm, and R. Beatty. 1972. *A Child's Garden: A Guide for Parents and Teachers.* Chevron Chem. Co., Ortho Div., San Francisco, Ca.

Douma, M. 1976. *Indoor Gardening in the Classroom.* The Penn. Hort. Soc., Philadelphia, Pa.

Finnegan, E. 1964. "Adventures in the vegetable kingdom." *Parent's Mag.* 39: 50-51.

Franz, M. 1969. "Three teen-age organic gardeners." *Org. Gard. & Farm.* 16: 52-56.

Garrett, B. 1975. "Fun gardening for kids." *Bet. Homes & Gard.* 53: 64-67.

Gjersvik, M. 1974. *Green Fun: Instant Toys, Tricks and Amusements Anyone Can Make from Common Weeds, Seeds, Leaves and Flowering Things.* Chatham Pr., Inc., New York

———. 1975. *Green Fun.* Chatham Pr., New York

Graham, A. and F. Graham. 1974. *Dooryard Garden: Tim and Jennifer's Calender From Planning to Harvesting.* Schol. Bk. Serv., Englewood Cliffs, N.J.

Johnson, F. 1969. "Green-thumb junior style." *Org. Gard. & Farm.* 16: 61.

Kempthorne, W. 1968. "Community garden for children: Jurupa Mountains Cultural Center, Riverside, California." *Am. Home* 71: 20

Kinney, R. R. 1955. *Guide to Gardening with Young People.* Prentice-Hall, Inc., Englewood Cliffs, N.J.

Kraft, K. and P. Kraft. 1970. "Victory gardens for vegetable-hating kids." *Today's Health* 48: 58-62.

Laking, L. 1964. "Garden for every child, Royal Botanical Gardens, Hamilton." *Flower Grower* 51: 36.

Meyer, H. G. 1965. "School gardens in Cleveland." *Horticulture* 43: 24-25.

Miner, F. M. 1951. "Fingers in the soil: Brooklyn Botanic Garden." *Recreation* 45: 98.

———. 1964. "The children's gardens in the Brooklyn Botanic Garden: a step to adulthood." *J. Roy. Hort. Soc.* 89:(6).

Paul, A. 1972. *Kids Gardening.* Doubleday & Co., Inc., New York

———. 1975. *Kids Indoor Gardening.* Archway Paperbacks, New York

Petrich, P. and R. Dalton. 1974. *The Kids's Garden Book.* Nitty Gritty Prods., Concord, Ca.

Price, T. 1975. "Plan a garden for your children." *Org. Gard. & Farm.* 22:

146-147.

Schatz, A. and V. Schatz. 1970. "Children's gardens in New York City schools: an educational report dated 1897." *Org. Gard. & Farm.* 17: 67-69.

Scobey, J. and N. Myers. 1975. *Gifts from Your Garden.* Bobbs-Merril Co., Inc., Indianapolis, Ind.

Shalucha, B. 1947. *A Walk through the Garden at Hilltop (Bloomington Youth Gardens).* Indiana Univ. Publs.

Skelsey, A. and G. Huckaby. 1973. *Growing Up Green: Parents and Children Gardening Together.* Workman Pub. Co., New York

Soucie, A. H. 1974. *Plant Fun: Ten Easy Plants to Grow Indoors.* Schol. Bk. Serv., Englewood Cliffs, N.J.

Sweningson, S. 1975. *Indoor Gardening.* Lerner Publs. Co., Minneapolis, Minn.

Van der Smissen, B. et al. 1968. *Leader's Guide to Nature-oriented Activities.* Iowa St. Univ. Pr., Ames, Ia.

Wendler, H. G. 1964. "Let's bring children into the garden." *Horticulture* 42: 36-37.

———. 1969. "Children's gardens keep them interested." *Horticulture* 47: 40-42.

Wotowiec, P. J. 1970. "Pioneer horticulture program in elementary schools." *Agric. Ed. Mag.* May: 278-279.

———. 1975. "Tips for a successful children's gardening program." *Org. Gard. & Farm.* 22: 116-119.

Zucker, I. 1964. "Children grow in gardens." *Gard.* 15: 34-35.

COLLECTING PLANT MATERIALS

Many inexpensive objects and decorations can be made from materials found in nature. The flower garden, the woods, fields, and roadsides are valuable sources. Collecting should begin early in the spring and continue through the late fall, but many collectibles are available all year round.

Collectibles

Berries: bayberry, bittersweet, holly, pyracantha, sumac

Cones: various evergreens

Nuts: acorns, beechnuts, chestnuts, hazelnuts, hickory, pecans, walnuts

Pits: apricot, avocado, cherry, date, peach, plum

Pods: alders, burdock, castorbean, catalpa, coffee tree, iris, locust, magnolias, mallows, maples, milkweeds, poppies,

roses, sensitive ferns, sweet gum, sweet pepperbush, syca-
more, tulip tree, witch hazel, yucca

Seeds: apple, barley, beans, corn, cucumber, gourds, grapefruit, lemon, lime, orange, peas, pumpkin, rice, squash,
sunflower, watermelon.

Collect bark, cork, decorative wood (drift, weathered, cross-
sections of tree trunks), fungi, leaves, lichens, lycopods, mosses,
mushrooms, shells, sea glass, sand, twigs, pebbles, and rocks.

Suggested Projects

Make wall plaques using a piece of wood, hooks, and dried
plant materials.

Use driftwood for flower and plant containers.

Make a collage with pieces of driftwood and shells.

For mobiles use coat hangers, nylon line, shells, and cones.

Make seed mosaics with plywood or cardboard, molding, seeds,
glue, acrylic spray, varnish or shellac.

For bird feeders use pine cones covered with peanut butter and
seeds.

To make pine cone flowers separate cone scales and arrange
them on plaques, or cut cones in cross-section, and attach a
piece of wire for a stem.

For jewelry make pins from pine cones and pits. Earrings can
be made from acorn cups.

Arrange dried materials on straw plates and hang on the walls
or doors.

Use dried lichens, moss, and fungi for miniature landscapes.

To make shadow boxes use small, shallow cans (sardine) to
make mini-shadow boxes. Use various dried plant materials.
Make mini-scenes and decorate the can.

To make greeting cards use dried materials. Overlap small
pieces of arborvitae in the shape of a Christmas tree.

Leaf ink prints can be made with paper, roller, and printer's ink.

Leaf spatter prints can be made with paper, brush, and ink.

Make miniature scenes in seashells.

Decorate flower pots with small seashells.

Use dried cornhusks to make cornhusk dolls.

Find rocks with depressions, and use these for planters and landscapes.

References

Alkema, C. J. 1972. *Crafting with Nature's Materials.* Sterling Pub. Co. Inc., New York

Bale, R. O. 1959. *Creative Nature Crafts.* Burgess Pub. Co., Minneapolis, Minn.

Benson, K. R. and C. E. Frankson. 1968. *Creative Nature Crafts.* Prentice-Hall, Inc., Englewood Cliffs, N.J.

Epple, A. O. 1974. *Start off in Nature Crafts.* Chilton Book Co., Radnor, Pa.

————. 1974. *Nature Crafts.* Chilton Book Co., Radnor, Pa.

Frazier, B. 1972. *Nature Crafts and Projects.* Troubador Pr., San Francisco, Ca.

Musselman, V. W. 1969. *Learning about Nature through Crafts.* Stackpole Books, Harrisburg, Pa.

Olman, A. E. 1975. *Mother Nature's Craft Book.* Pyramid Pubns. Inc., New York

COMMUNITY GARDENING

Community gardening is ideal for those who do not have enough land of their own or for those individuals that are living in disadvantaged areas and lack proper soil conditions. This kind of gardening is a group activity that enables people to share in a creative endeavor. It provides a learning situation that demonstrates the wonders of nature and teaches new skills.

Adequate planning is the key to success, and it should begin the fall before the group's first planting season. The location, size of plots, soil preparation, and layout must be considered at the start. There is no hard and fast rule concerning size, and this will vary depending on availability of space and demand. The plots are usually laid out in a grid pattern with 2 to 3 foot walkways between the plots. Stakes are used to define the corners or boundaries of each plot. Later, some type of fencing may be necessary to discourage vandalism and pilfering.

It is best to have a supervisor or site coordinator who will manage the project from preseason organization on through spring planting and summer care to fall clean up. Such a person may be an enthusiastic volunteer such as a senior citizen. Equally important is having a source of technical information available so that the participants can receive advice about their crops.

Because space is a limiting factor, the selection of plants is very important. Avoid crops such as corn, squash, pumpkins, and potatoes which take up a lot of space. Midget varieties of vegetables, and crops that can be trained to grow on trellises and that can be staked are ideal. Use the techniques of double planting, interplanting, and succession plantings to increase yield and to save space. Refer to the Activity Section — Vegetable Gardening and to Chapter Four: The Disadvantaged and Community Gardens for additional information.

References

Anonymous. 1975. "How to arrange a community vegetable garden." *Good House*. 180: 188.

Butler, G. D. 1967. *Introduction to Community Recreation*. McGraw-Hill Book Co., New York

Little, C. E. 1974. "Empty lots bloom in nation's cities." *Smithsonian* 5: 82-88.

Minnich, J. 1976. "To garden in the city, organize community plots." *House Beaut*. 118: 120-121.

Young, D. 1973. *Gardens for All: Guide to a Greener, Happier, Healthier Community*. Gardens for All, Inc., Charlotte, Vt.

DISH GARDENING

A dish garden is a miniature, scenic garden consisting of relatively slow-growing plants. A well-planned landscape, in addition to a suitable container and compatible plants, offers the opportunity to create an object of horticultural beauty.

A wide variety of containers can be used. Anything that will hold two inches of growing medium is satisfactory. Crockery, metal pans, glass containers, wooden boxes, small tubs, shells, sculptured feather rocks, old stumps and logs, bonsai dishes, ashtrays, clay and plastic saucers, and aluminum pie plates can be used. A rustic rock planter can be made in the following way:

1. Mix equal parts of Portland cement, vermiculite, and sphagnum peat moss (one part of perlite can also be added). Add one to one and one-half parts water and mix. The planter can also be colored by using lime-proof cement coloring powder. Use 1/2 cup to each quart of cement mixture.
2. Line a mold with a sheet of plastic. The mold may be a flower pot, an aluminum pie plate, or any other container. A large planter can be made by filling a cardboard carton with crushed paper in the shape of an oval. Place a sheet of plastic over the depression, and then spoon in the cement mixture.
3. Shape the cement mixture into the mold, pressing the bottom and sides.
4. Shape and press a piece of wire mesh screening against the molded cement mixture.
5. Add more cement mixture to the mold and press it against the wire mesh, covering it up completely.
6. Loosely cover the casting with a sheet of plastic. After twenty-four to forty-eight hours, remove the cast from the mold.
7. Over a one-week period, spray the cast with water or soak it in a solution of potassium permanganate to leach out any lime.
8. The cement mixture should be thoroughly dry within two weeks.
9. With a wire brush, scrape down the edges, corners, and the sides to give the appearance of natural rock.

Drainage material in a dish garden is very important. Use suitable material such as gravel or perlite. Use a basic soil mixture, but specialty plants such as cacti, succulents, orchids, and bromeliads will require special mixes.

Use upright plants in combination with spreading and training plants. Emphasize contrast by using plants of different colors and forms. Consider grasses, herbs, ground ivies, dwarf trees and shrubs, cacti, and succulents. Make sure that the plants are compatible with each other. Avoid drafts, heaters, or cold window sills. Do not overwater. Prune from time to time, and remove any dead leaves. Do not expect the garden to last indefinitely.

Follow the flower arranging principles of line, proportion, and balance. Base a design on a theme such as an alpine landscape, a Japanese garden, or a woodland scene. Use small tools, and improvise by using kitchen spoons, forks, and chopsticks. Use a mister or sprayer to water the garden.

Use accent materials such as pebbles, bark, lichens, moss, pocket mirrors for reflecting pools, and fungi. Employ terraces, ledges, and rolling hills for contrast and depth. Select the tallest plant or an accessory object, and arrange the plants around it, finishing with the ground covers.

Suggested Plantings

To plant in spiral seashells, use long-stranded sphagnum moss as the planting medium. Wrap the roots in moist moss, and tuck it into the shell. Water by placing the shell in water, and drain off any excess. Fertilize with a weak solution of fertilizer every second or third watering.

Plant cacti and succulents in ceramic containers or in shells.

Use woodland plants in a wooden box or tray accented with driftwood and lichens.

Plant dwarf conifers and *Sedum* for a mini-alpine scene.

Use miniature plants in tiny bonsai containers.

Plant herbs in ceramic or clay containers for the kitchen.

Plant various house plants in clear brandy snifters and in open globes.

Plant woodland plants on and in depressions of tufa stone.

Plant succulents and cacti in depressions of feather or lava stone. First soak the rock in water to make it easier to work with. Chisel lightly with a hammer into the desired shape. Fill the depressions with a suitable soil mix. Cover the bottom of the rock with felt or cork to prevent the scratching of tabletops. Use cacti, succulents, peperomias, African violets, and orchids.

References

Beard, P. 1930. *Adventures in Dish Gardening.* A. T. De La Mare Company, Inc., New York
Kramer, J. 1975. *Miniature Gardens in Bowl, Dish and Tray.* Charles Scribner's Sons, Totawa, N.J.

DRYING PLANTS AND FLOWERS

Dried plant materials are those whose moisture has been removed to assure that they will last indefinitely. They can be used for arrangements, for bouquets, and for other displays. The main objectives are for color, artistic shape, and for decorative value.

Color

The natural color can be retained if the right method is used. The following is a list of plant materials that can be dried for their color:

Red: cockscomb, peony, pomegranate, roses, strawflowers, sumac, zinnia

Pink: delphinium, gladiolus, globe amaranth, larkspur, peony, snapdragon, statice

Yellow: acacia, chrysanthemum, goldenrod, marigold, strawflower, yarrow, zinnia

Blue: cornflower, delphinium, globe thistle, hydrangea, larkspur, salvia

Green: ferns, foliage, grasses, hydrangea, seed pods

Orange: bittersweet, chinese lanterns, marigolds, strawflower,

zinnia
    Violet: gladiolus, heather, lilac, statice, stock
    Gray: artemisia, bayberry, dusty miller
    Brown: canna, cones, dock, seed pods
    Tan: grasses, leaves, seed pods, wood roses
    Black: baptisia pods, magnolia leaves, teasel
    White: baby's breath, honesty, peony, Queen Anne's Lace,
statice, strawflower

Techniques

The Hanging Method

Small, compact flowers dry well using this method.

1. Collect the plants on a bright, sunny day before they reach full maturity, but not after their color begins to deteriorate.
2. Remove all unnecessary leaves. The shaping of the plants can also be done at this time. The original stem can be removed and replaced with florist's wire inserted through the bottom of the floral head.
3. Tie the plants in small bunches and suspend them upside down. This keeps the stems straight and the flower heads upright.
4. Hang the plants in a dry, warm location with good ventilation. Do not cover or enclose them in a closet. Do not expose them to direct sun.

It takes about eight to ten days for the majority of plants to dry, but this depends upon humidity. The plants will go through various stages of wilting. During this process, there is some shrinkage, and the bunch will have to be tightened. The plants are dry when the leaves and stems are crisp. The following plants can be dried in this way:

baby's breath, bells-of-Ireland, bittersweet, cattails, Chinese lanterns, cockscomb, dock, everlasting, globe amaranth, goldenrod, herbs, lilac seed heads, milkweed pods, mullein, pampas grass, pepper grass, rhododendron seed heads, sensitive fern, statice, steeple bush, strawberry corn, strawflowers, sumac, wild carrot, wild grasses, yarrow.

THE AGENT METHOD

Some materials do not retain their color and shape if they are dried by the hanging method, and therefore, various drying agents must be used. These include cornstarch, powdered sugar, fuller's earth, alum, silica gel, powdered pumice, salt, borax, sand, and cornmeal. One commonly used mixture is one part borax and one part cornmeal. To each quart of this mixture, three tablespoons of salt are added. It takes about a week in this mixture, whereas it takes three to five weeks in pure sand.

The flowers are collected on a dry day. Put them in water for about an hour to prevent wilting during the first stage of drying. Pour 1 inch of the drying mixture in a box. Place the flowers (head down) on top of the mixture. Gently sift the agent over and around the flowers. Check after one week, and if they are dry, lift them carefully from the mixture, and remove any clinging grains with a brush. A slight modification is to place the flowers in a paper bag with agent covering them. Tie the bag around the stem and gently shake the bag so that the agent will reach all parts. Flowers left in borax mixtures after they have dried tend to lose their color, so remove the flowers as soon as they have dried. The following flowers dry well in agents:

baptisia, chrysanthemums, clover, cosmos, daffodils, daisy, delphinium, hollyhocks, hydrangea, larkspur, love-in-a-mist, lunaria, Mexican sunflower, marigolds, roses, salvia, snapdragons, teasel, thistle, zinnias.

GLYCERIN METHOD FOR FOLIAGE

To preserve color and flexibility in foliage, immerse the branches in a solution of one part glycerin to two parts water for twenty-four hours. For thicker leaves such as magnolia, boxwood, and rhododendrons, the process takes three weeks.

PRESSING PLANT MATERIALS

Insert plant material between pieces of absorbent paper or in heavy books (telephone books) with tissue paper over and under the plants. The plants should not touch each other. A weight such as a brick is placed on the book. The tissues should be changed every eight hours for the first twenty-four hours. The material should dry for two to three weeks. Single-petaled flowers work the best.

Selected Activities

POTPOURRI

A potpourri is a small "compost" of exquisite ingredients such as flower petals, oils, spices, gums, barks, and leaves. It is used to refresh and scent the air.

Start to collect the ingredients during the summer and throughout the fall. The flowers should be selected for their color and fragrance. Rose petals are commonly used because they retain some of their fragrance. The petals of carnations, geraniums, heliotrope, honeysuckle, lavender, lilac and spice pinks can also be used. Separate the petals and place them on newspapers to dry. Mix them two or three times a day to hasten drying. After the petals are "crackle" dry, sprinkle them with salt, orrisroot or gum benzoin (preservatives), various spices, and brown sugar. Layers of the ingredients are placed in a jar, and these are aged for three to six weeks. The mixture should be mixed twice a week. Once blended, the mixture will last for years. The following are some potpourri recipes:

General Mixture
1 gallon dried flower petals
1 box plain salt
1 tablespoon allspice
1 ounce oil of bergamot
1/2 ounce orrisroot powder
Small box of ground cinnamon
1 box bay leaves

Mint Potpourri
2 cups dried lavender
1 cup dried mint leaves (peppermint, spearmint, orangemint)
1/2 cup dried thyme
1/4 cup rosemary
A few drops of lavender, thyme, and bergamot oil
Dried red geranium petals, blue bachelor's buttons, and delphiniums

Kitchen Potpourri
1 quart pineapple or regular sage leaves
1 quart rosemary
2 cups thyme
1 cup oregano
1 cup sweet basil
1 1/2 ounces orrisroot powder
1 teaspoon powdered ginger

Mountain Mixture
1 quart pine needles
1 quart juniper berries
1 cup parsley
1 ounce orrisroot powder
2 teaspoons sweet basil
2 teaspoons sage

SACHET

Dried petals and leaves are mixed in a small case made of a porous fabric such as cheesecloth, satin, or net. They are placed in dresser drawers or among linens. Lavender is commonly used. Mix equal parts of carnations, spice pink petals, rose geranium leaves, and a few cornflowers for color. Mix rose petals or rose geraniums with mint blossoms. Properly prepared materials will hold their fragrance for years.

POMANDER BALL

Cloves are inserted into a fresh orange, and a small quantity of powdered cinnamon is placed in a bag with the orange and shaken. Then, place the orange in a dry, dark location for ten days. It becomes a firm, fragrant ball which will keep its spicy odor for a long time. It can be hung in a closet as a sachet.

FLORAL PRINTS

Use construction paper, velvet, satin, or burlap for the background. Pressed flowers are mounted and glued on one at a time. The picture can be covered with clear plastic or glass.

PLACEMATS AND BOOKMARKERS

Arrange pressed plant material on a piece of plastic Contac paper. Apply another piece of plastic over the arrangement. The margins can be cut with pinking shears.

DRIED FLOWER ARRANGEMENTS

Plan to dry at least a dozen of each floral variety. Arrangements of one or two flowers of many varieties do not look as effective as a mass of four or five kinds. Use dried leaves, branches, and ferns for fillers. Use oasis, Styrofoam, sand, or clay to support the plants in the container.

CALICO CORN

The kernels can be softened with water and strung to make necklaces. The kernels can also be used to make seed mosaics. Calico corn comes in various colors: striped quadricolor, squaw or Indian Corn, and gracilis (a dwarf variety).

DRYING GOURDS

Gourds come in a great variety of shapes, sizes, and colors. They are very attractive as centerpieces and as hanging decorations. The dipper variety makes a handy dipper, and the bird's nest gourd can be used to make a birdhouse. Some of the larger gourds can be used for flower pots. There are aromatic gourds (queen pocket melon), and the Japanese bottle luffa gourd has an inner fibrous mass that makes an excellent bath sponge.

Only fully matured, but not overly ripened gourds will dry in good condition. A gourd is ripe when it detaches from the vine with a slight twist. To dry gourds, the gourd is removed from the vine with a portion of the stem still attached. Remove all soil, but be careful not to damage the outer skin. To prevent the growth of mold and fungus, immerse the gourd in a disinfectant before drying. Make a hole in each end of the gourd about the size of a hatpin needle. This assures proper ventilation during the drying process. Depending on the size of the gourd, the process takes from one to six months. They are dry when the seeds rattle inside when shaken. The gourd can be decorated with shells, paint or wax.

References

Amlick, B. A. 1971. *Getting Started in Dried Flower Craft*. Bruce Pub. Co., Riverside, N.J.

Bauzen, P. and S. Bauzen. 1971. *Flower Pressing*. Sterling Pub. Co., Inc., New York

Bugbee, A. S. 1975. *How to Dry Flowers The Easy Way*. Houghton Mifflin Co., Boston, Ma.

Derbyshire, J. and R. Burgess. 1975. *Arco Book of Dried and Pressed Flowers*. Arco Pub. Co., Inc., New York

Eaton, M. 1973. *Flower Pressing*. Lerner Pubns. Co., Minneapolis, Minn.

Floyd, H. 1973. *Plant It Now, Dry It Later*. McGraw-Hill Book Co., New York

Foster, L. L. 1970. *Keeping the Plants You Pick*. Thomas Y. Crowell Co., New York

Foster, M. 1974. *Preserved Flowers: Practical Methods and Creative Uses*. Transatlantic Arts Inc., Levittown, New York

Lutz, E. L. 1971. *How to Embed Flowers in Plastic*. Naturegraph Pubs., Healdsburg, Ca.

Morrison, W. 1975. *Drying and Preserving Flowers*. Hippocrene Books, Inc., New York

Shipman, D. and M. McWilliam. 1975. *Everlasting Flowercraft*. Arco Publishing Co., Inc., New York

Squires, M. 1958. *The Art of Drying Plants and Flowers*. Bonanza Books, New York

Stevenson, V. 1972. *Dried Flowers For Decoration.* David & Charles, Inc., North Pomfret, Vt.

Tucker, A. 1972. *Potpourri, Incense and Other Fragrant Concoctions.* Workman Pub. Co., Inc., New York

Wach, N. 1975. *The Elegant Art of Pressing and Preserving Seeds, Leaves and Flowers.* C. R. Gibson Co., Norwalk, Conn.

Wagner, L. 1974. *How to Have Fun Pressing Flowers.* Creative Ed. Soc. Inc., Mankato, Minn.

Whitlock, S. and M. Rankin. 1975. *Dried Flowers: How to Prepare and Arrange Them.* Dover Pubns. Inc., New York

ECOLOGY BOXES

An ecology box is a type of "shadow box" or windowed box that displays an ecological theme such as the seashore, woodland, or desert. The box is partitioned into various cubicles, each displaying a particular object or objects. One cubicle may contain seeds or dried flowers, another, sand or soil, and another, a pine cone. It may be a garden theme, a cereal theme, or a food theme. It may be a mixture of objects with no particular theme at all and called a "memory box."

The box can be constructed from cardboard, wood, or plastic. It can be any size or shape, and the window can be plastic, glass, or cellophane. Even old cigar boxes that have been partitioned may be used. These windowed boxes have become a popular craft, and they are excellent conversation pieces.

The following steps are for making a box out of wood:

1. Use two different widths of lattice, one 1/4 inch narrower than the other. Use the wider lattice for the outside frame and the narrower lattice for the inside frame and the partitions. Plan all outside and inside dimensions, and then measure how much lattice is needed.
2. The back of the box can be of composition board, plywood, or heavy cardboard. Decide on the overall size of the box, and cut the back to fit.
3. Cut the wider lattice first. Cut two sections to fit the width of the back, and glue the lattice (standing on its edge) flush with the back width. The box can be nailed together, but an epoxy glue is more convenient. Cut two more sec-

tions of the wider lattice to fit the length of the backboard, and glue them between the lattice already attached to the back.

4. A smaller frame is made with the narrower lattice; this is fitted inside the outer lattice frame. Glue the inner lattice frame to the back as well as to the sides of the outer lattice frame.

5. Cut the inside vertical and horizontal cross-walls from the narrow lattice. Glue in place.

6. Fill the spaces with dried materials, seeds, seashells, and other objects.

7. Place a pane of glass into the box so that it rests on the inner frame.

8. Cut screen molding to form a frame to fit on top of the outer lattice walls. The molding can be cut into two widths and two lengths, or it can be cut with mitered corners.

9. Glue the molding over the top of the outer frame to hold the glass in place. The frame may be varnished or painted. Wall hangers can then be attached.

Suggested Projects

Use old window frames that are deep set for ecology boxes.

California Job Cases (printer's cases) already have numerous cubicles, and these make very impressive ecology boxes.

Old drawers from kitchen tables and plastic trays with partitions can also be used to make ecology boxes.

Use empty gift boxes that contained various cheeses, jellies, and cookies; these boxes already have the partitions and are ready-made ecology boxes.

FLOWER ARRANGING

This activity offers a medium for artistic self-expression and relaxation. Young and old alike can learn to make a flower arrangement.

The key to successful flower arranging is a knowledge of the basic artistic principles, elements of design, and color harmonies. The elements of design include line, form, pattern, texture, and color. *Line* is the basic skeleton of the arrangement, and it may be vertical, horizontal, triangular, or radial. *Form* consists of the three-dimensional shape of the arrangement. *Pattern* is the outline the arrangement makes against space. *Texture* and *color* are qualities that make an arrangement interesting and appealing. The way lines are arranged creates *balance*. Balance makes the design look stable. The highest point of the arrangement should be directly or close to the focal point. Dark-colored, large, and coarse textured flowers are placed low and near the center whereas light-colored, small, and fine textured flowers are placed toward the edges. Smaller flowers can be massed together to form one larger one. All parts should contribute to the *rhythm* or rhythmic movement of the eye along the design. This effect can be obtained by using several flowers of the same color or shape, or by using the same flower in different sizes. Avoid crossed stems that interfere with the sweeping motion of the eye. All parts of the arrangement should be in *scale*. This includes the flowers, the foliage, the container, and the background. A general rule is that the flowers and foliage should be one and one-half times as high as the container. All lines in the design should converge at a *focal point*. This is usually low and in the center and may be accented by using a sharp contrast in form, size, or color. All parts should be in *harmony*. This involves the blending of color, texture, shape, and design. All should complement each other. *Repetition* of form, texture, color, and kinds of plant material results in *unity*. All parts should belong to the arrangement. This is achieved by limiting the arrangement to a small number of flowers of a few different types.

Three main types of flowers used in arrangements are spikes, buttons, and background flowers.

Spikes: These have a narrow, straight look and pointed tips. They are put in the arrangement first and form the outline. Examples are gladiolus, snapdragon, stock, delphinium, roses, iris, celosia, pussy willow, lilac, and heads of grain.

Buttons: These are round in shape and are used to create an accent or focus, and to break space into interesting patterns. They are placed in the arrangement after the spikes. Examples are zinnias, marigolds, open roses, petunias, carnations, chrysanthemums, camellias, daisies, and gardenias.

Background: These have fine textures and irregular outlines. They add lightness and airiness to an arrangement. They are not as essential as the other two, and they are used sparingly. Examples are baby's breath, statice, asparagus fern, heather, and love-in-a-mist.

Greenery: Use ferns, cuttings from shrubs, and ground covers.

Materials: Flower holders (chicken wire, pin or needle holders, oasis, moist sand, vermiculite, shredded Styrofoam), florist's wire to strengthen stems, floral tape to secure oasis in the container, sharp knife or scissors, suitable containers (bowls 8 inches across and 3 inches deep are ideal), clay to anchor pin holders in the container.

Conditioning: Condition the flowers before arranging them by placing them in a container filled with warm water and place them in a cool (50° F), dark area for a few hours or overnight. Remove all foliage below the waterline, and cut the stem at an angle. For best results, cut the flowers in the late afternoon or early evening.

Making an Arrangement

Envision a shape for the arrangement. It may be a formally balanced triangle or informal bouquet. It may be circular, oval, or crescent shaped. The design may take an *S* curve or follow a basic vertical or horizontal line. An easy design to make is a modified triangle:

1. Cut the oasis to size and soak it in water for one-half hour, and then secure it to the container with floral tape.
2. Insert spike-like flowers first. The tallest spike will go in first, and its height should be one and one-half times the width of the container. Place this spike toward the back. Then cut a slightly shorter spike and place this to the

right of the first and slightly forward. The third spike is shorter than the second, and it is positioned to form a triangle.

3. Next, insert the button flowers. These should alternate with the spikes, and be placed at various levels. Rotate and work on all sides.
4. Place background or filler flowers between the button flowers, and also fill in with greenery around the bottom and back to cover the mechanics.
5. Keep the arrangement in a cool place at night, and change the water daily. Never expose the arrangement to direct sun or drafts.

Suggested Projects

Make a temporary underwater or submerged arrangement. Roses and sweet peas will survive submerging, and these may be displayed in crystal jars or globes. A strip of lead around the stem will anchor the flowers.

Arrange flowers in a clear glass container filled with crystal marbles or sea glass.

Consider arranging various vegetables and fruits with flowers, especially around Thanksgiving.

For a Christmas arrangement, use red roses with juniper, holly, pine, or other evergreens.

For Valentine's Day, use red roses, white camellias, scented violets, and red and white carnations.

For Easter, use lilies, spring-flowering bulbs, lilac, and blooming shrubs.

Do not neglect the common wildflowers such as daisies, goldenrod, and Queen Anne's lace.

Make miniature arrangements in bottle caps for children.

Arrange miniature dried or fresh flowers in egg shells. This is an ideal activity for children around Easter time.

References

Allen, E. G. 1965. *Japanese Flower Arrangement in a Nutshell*. Charles E. Tuttle Co., Rutland, Vt.

Clements, J. 1963. *A Hundred and One Ideas for Flower Arrangement*. D. Van Nostrand Co., Inc., Princeton, N.J.

Hillier, F. B. 1974. *Basic Guide to Flower Arranging*. McGraw-Hill Book Co., New York

Ishimoto, T. 1951. *The Art of Driftwood and Dried Arrangements*. Crown Pubs., Inc., New York

Nehrling, A. and I. Nehrling. 1969. *Flower Growing For Flower Arrangement*. Hearthside Press, Inc., New York

Piercy, H. 1971. *Dried Flowers for Winter Arrangements*. British Heritage and Jonathan Cape, London

Roberts, P. E. 1958. *How to Make Flower Decorations*. The Studio Pubns., Inc., New York

Rockwell, F. F. and E. C. Grayson. 1960. *The Rockwell's New Complete Book of Flower Arrangement*. Doubleday & Co., Inc., New York

Seibel, W. E. 1961. *Arts and Crafts for Flower Arrangers*. D. Van Nostrand, Inc., Princeton, N.J.

Smith, J. E. 1967. *Flower Arranging: A Manual*. Lucas Bros. Pubs., Columbia, Mo.

Underwood, R. M. 1962. *The Complete Book of Dried Arrangements*. Bonanza Books, New York

FLOWER GARDENING

A display of brilliantly colored and fragrant flowers is a pleasure to the senses and the soul. The flower garden, bed, or border may be of any size or shape. It may serve as a hospital garden that is specially designed for the use of wheelchair and semiambulatory patients.

Flower gardens usually include annuals, biennials, and perennials. The plants are arranged according to their height with the tallest in the background or in the center, and those of medium height and border plants toward the front and sides. This arrangement will give a well-ordered appearance, and allows proper light for each plant. Vary or scatter the height lines for charm, and plant in groups rather than in rows. When selecting plants, consider their color and blooming periods. The garden should get full sun, and if the soil needs to be fertilized, apply 2 pounds of 5-10-5 per 100 square foot. If shade is a problem, select plants such as impatiens, begonias, and coleus.

Annuals

Annuals are plants that complete their life cycle in one growing season. When many of the perennials stop flowering, the annuals just begin. Some easy to grow annuals are the following:
African daisy, ageratum, anchusa, balsam, calendula, candytuft, China aster, cleome, cockscomb, coreopsis, cosmos, flowering tobacco, forget-me-not, four o'clock, larkspur, marigold, nasturtium, petunia, portulaca, sunflower, sweet alyssum, verbena, and zinnia.

FRAGRANT ANNUALS

Chinese pink, drummond phlox, heliotrope, jasmine tobacco, mignonette, nasturtium, pansy, purple candytuft, rocket larkspur, scabiosa, snapdragon, stock, sweet alyssum, sweet pea, sweet sultan, verbena, yellow lupine

ANNUALS FOR CUT FLOWERS

calliopsis, China aster, Chinese pink, chrysanthemum, cornflower, cosmos, marigold, pansy, scalloped salpiglossis, snapdragon, sweet pea, sweet scabiosa, sweet sultan, zinnia

To start annuals from seed, sow the seeds indoors in March and April and outdoors in May. See Table II for cultivation requirements for some common annual flowers.

Biennials

These plants produce top growth the first season and flowers and seed during the second season. In practice, biennials are treated as annuals. Most are purchased commercially with the first year's growth already behind them. Some biennials are Canterbury Bells, English Daisy, Foxglove, Hollyhock, Honesty, Iceland Poppy, Pansy, Siberian Wallflower, and Sweet William.

Perennials

Perennial plants are adapted to hard winters and are perpetuated from year to year by underground roots, bulbs, tubers, corms, and rhizomes. They are also easily grown from seed, coming into bloom the second year after being sown. Sow the seeds outdoors in spring, late summer, or early fall. Some easy-to-grow perennials are:
achillea, astilbe, beebalm, bleeding-heart, columbine, coral bells, coreopsis, daylily, geum, hosta, lily-of-the-valley, loose-strife, lychnis, oriental poppy, shasta daisy, and sedum.

Perennials should be divided every three to four years. The general rule is to divide the spring and early summer perennials in the fall, and the late summer bloomers in the spring. When the perennials cease flowering, plant the annuals to replace them in the flower garden.

A Special Project — A Hospital Garden

A hospital garden can be adjacent to a building so that the patients have easy access to it. It may be an extension of a patio or terrace, or it may be within an enclosed atrium. If a terrace or patio is used, plant in tubs or barrels, and use numerous window boxes.

A larger hospital garden may be designed not only for aesthetic appeal, but also for direct patient participation. Design the garden so that the paths are 4 to 6 feet wide. The paths should also be paved or blacktopped so that wheelchairs and those on crutches can easily maneuver in the garden. Benches at various locations provide for relaxation within the garden. A few raised garden plots may also be used for contrast and for those in wheelchairs. Also include bird feeders and a pool if resources are available. A protected or enclosed area is suggested for meditation.

Select plant material that will interest the patients. Small trees, shrubs, and evergreens will provide for a year-round garden. Plant annuals and perennials that are colorful, fragrant, and that can be used for cut flowers later in the season.

Table II: Cultivation Requirements For Some Annual Flower Seeds

Flower	Germinating Temperature	Sow Seeds About	Days to Germinate	Transplant About	No. weeks from Seed to planting
Ageratum	70	Mar. 20	5-10	Apr. 20	8-10
Alyssum	70	Mar. 10	5-10	Apr. 20	8-10
Amaranthus	70	Apr. 20	8-10	May 10	4-6
Aster	70	Apr. 20	7-10	May 10	6-8
Balsam	80	Apr. 10	7-10	May 5	6-8
Bachelor's Buttons	70	Mar. 5	7-14	Mar. 25	12-16
Begonia	70	Mar. 5	14-35	Apr. 5	10-16
Cleome	70	Apr. 15	7-14	May 10	8-10
Celosia	70	Apr. 10	7-10	Apr. 25	4-6
Coleus	60	Apr. 5	10-14	Apr. 25	6-8
Cosmos	75	Apr. 25	5-10	May 10	6-8
Dusty Miller	65	Mar. 5	14-21	Apr. 5	10-12
Geraniums	75	Feb. 5	5-10	Mar. 5	18
Impatiens	70	Mar. 10	12-18	Apr. 5	9-12
Lobelia	70	Mar. 15	14-21	Apr. 15	9-12
Marigold	70	Apr. 10	5-7	Apr. 20	7-10
Nasturtium	65	Apr. 15	6-8	May 5	6-8
Petunia	70	Mar. 15	4-12	Apr. 15	10-12
Portulaca	70	Apr. 5	10-18	Apr. 25	6-8
Strawflower	65-70	Mar. 5	7-14	Apr. 5	12-14
Verbena	65	Mar. 10	14-28	Apr. 10	8-10
Zinnia	70	Apr. 25	5-10	May 10	4-6

References

Askwith, H. (ed.). 1961. *The Complete Guide to Garden Flowers*. A. S. Barnes and Co., New York

Bloom, A. 1974. *Perennials for Your Garden*. Charles Scribner's Sons, Totowa, N.J.

Crockett, J. U. 1971. *Annuals*. Time-Life Books, New York

———. 1972. *Perennials*. Time-Life Books, New York

Schuler, S. 1975. *The Gardener's Basic Book of Flowers*. Simon & Schuster, Inc., New York

Shewell-Cooper, W. E. 1975. *Basic Book of Flower Gardening*. Drake Pubs.,

Inc., New York

Sunset Editors. 1974. *How to Grow and Use Annuals*. Lane Books, Menlo Park, Ca.

FORCING BULBS

The "bulb" plants include those grown from corms, tubers, and bulbs. These include tulips, lilies, daffodils, crocus, scillas, hyacinths, and paper-white narcissus. For most bulbs, the process of forcing involves a low temperature (50° F) and slow growth (10-12 weeks).

Guidelines

1. The secret for success is a pot full of roots. The roots must be developed before any other growth. This is achieved by removing all light and by maintaining a temperature of about 50° to 60° F.
2. Slow growth should precede bloom. Bulbs placed in direct sunlight immediately after being in the dark develop too fast. In this case, the foliage falls over, and the stems are weak. Keep the plants in the shade for a few days.
3. It is always best to buy quality bulbs. Select firm bulbs that are free of blemishes. Some dealers offer bulbs already prepared for forcing. These "preforced" bulbs have previously been subjected to a cool phase.

Forcing Bulbs in Pots

1. Bulbs to be forced are potted from October to December.
2. Clay pots are preferred, but plastic and peat pots can also be used. The only requirement is that they have proper drainage and that they be at least twice as deep as the bulb. A clean pot is essential, and new clay pots should be soaked overnight before being used.
3. Proper drainage is very important. Place a shard over the drainage hole, and add 1/2 inch of gravel or crushed stone.
4. Use a soil mixture of one part sand, one part peat moss,

and one part loam. Add 1 tablespoon of bonemeal or superphosphate per 6-inch pot. Avoid fresh manure or rich fertilizers because the bulbs store all the food they require to bloom.

5. There should be a minimum of 2 inches of soil below the bulbs. The tops of the bulbs should just be showing above the surface of the soil, and 1/2 inch below the rim of the container. The number of bulbs in a pot will depend on the size of the bulbs and on the size of the pot. Fill the pot with as many bulbs as possible for the fullest effect. The bulbs should be firm, especially around the base. Any accessory bulblets should be removed with the exception of narcissus. Tulips should be planted with the flat side of the bulb on the outside so that the first leaf will develop over the rim. After planting the bulbs, water the pot thoroughly by immersing the pot up to its rim in a pan of water.

6. Dig a trench 18 inches deep, place a layer of gravel on the bottom, and set the pots on this layer. Cover the pots with 4 to 6 inches of sand or peat moss. Then, fill in the trench with soil. Mulch with about a foot of leaves or 6 inches of peat moss held in place with boards. Wire mesh can be placed over the top to keep rodents away, and the trench may also be covered with a sheet of plastic to keep it dry.

7. During the rooting period, the temperature should be kept as close to 50° F as possible. Root development takes eight weeks for miniature hyacinths, ten to twelve weeks for hyacinths, ten to twelve weeks for tulips, and twelve to fifteen weeks for narcissus. After twelve weeks, check for root and shoot development. If the roots are protruding from the drainage hole, and the shoot is 1-1 1/2 inches, the pot should be taken indoors and placed in a cool location (50-60° F). During the first week, the pots should be placed in a shaded area, and gradually exposed to increased temperature and light. Water, if necessary, by immersing the pot up to its rim in water. Try to keep the pots at 55-60° F for the first month. The bulbs should flower four to six weeks after they are removed from the trench.

Suggested Projects

Autumn crocus (Colchicum autumnale)

It is very simple to force this bulb. Simply place the bulb on a sunny windowsill, or in a bowl with or without soil or water.

Paper-white Narcissus (Narcissus tazetta papyraceus)

These bulbs produce very fragrant flowers, and they can be forced early for Thanksgiving or Christmas. They do not need a cold period, and they can be forced in water.

1. Fill a deep bowl with pebbles, perlite, gravel, fiber, or a sandy soil to a depth of two inches.
2. Place the bulbs on the medium and push them slightly downwards so that the lower third of the bulb is covered with the media.
3. Add water up to the root crown of the bulbs, and refill when necessary.
4. Place the bowl in a dark, cool place until the foliage is 4 to 5 inches high, and then, move it to a warmer location. Flowering time is approximately six to eight weeks after planting. Too much sun, too much heat, and very dry air may cause the papery sheaths around the bulbs to dry, and this results in bud blast. If this occurs, mist the sheaths with water to keep them moist and pliable.

References

Miles, B. 1963. *The Wonderful World of Bulbs.* D. Van Nostrand Co., Inc., Princeton, N.J.

Selsam, M. E. 1974. *Bulbs, Corms, and Such.* Morrow, Wm. & Co., Inc., New York

Sunset Editors. 1973. *How to Grow Bulbs.* Lane Pub. Co., Menlo Park, Ca.

Walker, M. C. 1965. *Flowering Bulbs for Winter Windows.* D. Van Nostrand Co. Inc., Princeton, N.J.

Wister, G. S. 1964. *Hardy Garden Bulbs.* E. P. Dutton & Co. Inc., New York

FORCING FLOWERING BRANCHES

Flowering branches forced in water can brighten up the winter months. They can also be used to make arrangements.

The process takes very little time, and it is easy to do.

The early blossoming varieties are the easiest to force. Failures in forcing are caused by haste. Branches brought immediately into the heat begin a weak, scattered blossoming and dry up before full bloom is complete. In addition, the forcing process must not begin until the branches have been exposed to at least eight weeks of temperatures below 40° F. The procedure is as follows:

1. Use long branches; the longer the branch, the better the bloom. Crush the lower most two inches of the branch. Immerse at least 8 inches of the base of the branches into tepid water (not hot!) for a day. Then, place in a sunny window of a cool room (60-65° F) for about a week. Spray the branches each day with warm water.
2. When the buds are about to burst, bring them into a warmer room.
3. Refill and replace the water, and add a little charcoal to the water to keep it sweet. Periodically, cut off a piece of the base of the branch to keep water-conducting vessels open.
4. The blossoms will last longer if the branches are kept cool. When blooming ends, the leaves will appear.

Branches that are commonly forced are the following:
alders, almond (flowering), apple, azalea, cherry (flowering), deutzia, dogwood, forsythia, honeysuckles, lilac, magnolia, maple (Japanese and red), peach, pear, plum, pussy willow, quince, red bud, rhododendron, spicebush, spirea (bridal wreath), wisteria, and witch hazel.

Most shrubs can be cut for forcing in mid-February to early- and mid-March. Forcing time for most takes from three to five weeks, but the closer to the normal flowering time you begin the forcing process, the quicker the branches will flower.

References

Crockett, J. U. 1972. *Flowering Shrubs.* Time-Life Books, New York
Hersey, J. 1974. *Flowering Shrubs and Small Trees.* Charles Scribner's Sons, Totowa, N.J.

GARDENING IN CONTAINERS

Growing vegetables, herbs, and other plants in containers can be fun, and it also saves space. The containers can be conveniently placed on a patio, terrace, doorstep, or even on a rooftop. The advantages include less work, less bending, and the growing conditions can be controlled. However, this type of gardening requires more watering, more fertilizing, and occasional repotting.

The containers must be large enough to accommodate the root systems of the plants. Use containers with a 6 to 8 inch diameter for annuals and perennials planted singly; 10 to 12 inch containers for large perennials, vines, and larger vegetables; 12 to 18 inch containers for small shrubs; and 18 to 24 inch containers for medium-size shrubs and trees.

The container should be sturdy, have proper drainage, and be about as deep as it is wide. Use clay or plastic pots, wooden tubs or boxes, barrels, concrete tubs, old pails, bushel baskets, and plastic trash pails. Large plastic bags and burlap bags can also be used. Try planting a potato plant in a burlap bag filled with soil, and then harvest the potatoes already in the bag.

The soil mixture will depend on the plants, but the Cornell peat mix and other synthetic mixtures (soilless) are ideal because of their light weight. Use 1/2 to 1 inch of gravel for drainage.

Repot the plant when it is root bound. Place the plant into a container 1 inch wider and 1 inch deeper than the original container. Try not to loosen the soil around the sides of the root ball, but do remove any drainage material that may be stuck to the bottom. Add fresh soil, a little fertilizer, and water thoroughly. Fertilize with one level teaspoon of 5-10-5 per square foot of medium, once every three to four weeks.

Remember that plants growing in containers dry out faster. Mulching the surfaces helps to retain moisture, or sink the container into another larger container lined with peat moss.

Suggested Plants

Vegetables: A box two feet square by two feet deep can grow four tomato plants, each capable of yielding 25 pounds of fruit during the growing season. Peppers, cabbage, cucumbers, and lettuce are all suitable. Try the various dwarf and mini-varieties.

Flowering annuals: ageratum, impatiens, lobelia, marigold, myosotis, petunia, phlox, sweet alyssum, sweet peas (dwarf)

Flowering perennials: begonia, hosta, and various ferns. Cacti and succulents are ideal because they need less water and fertilizer and grow well in shallow containers.

Shrubs and trees: andromeda, azalea, camellia, Chinese hibiscus, citrus, fuchsia, gardenia, holly, hydrangea, Japanese maple, juniper, lantana, natal plum, Norfolk Island pine, oleander, olive, palm, peach, pine, podocarpus, pomegranate, rhododendron, roses, spruce, sweet bay.

References

Fenton, D. X. 1969. *Plants for Pots: Projects for Indoor Gardeners.* Lippincott, J. B. Co., New York

Kramer, J. 1971. *Container Gardening, Indoors and Out.* Doubleday & Co., Inc., New York

Mabe, R. E. 1974. *Rooftop and Patio Vegetable Gardening.* Potpourri Press, Greensboro, N.C.

McDonald, E. 1975. *Gardening in Containers.* Grosset & Dunlop, Inc., New York

Sunset Editors. 1967. *Gardening in Containers.* Lane Books, Menlo Park, Ca.

Taloumis, G. 1972. *Container Gardening Outdoors.* Simon and Schuster, Inc., New York

GARDENING IN RAISED BEDS

The use of raised beds is an attractive way to garden, and it is a very successful project for the disabled. A raised bed is a garden above the ground level that is held in place by low walls. They may be built against a wall, a fence, or a hedge. They may also be used for barriers or dividers. The walls of a raised bed protect the plants from weeds, roots, dogs, and traffic. They reduce labor and add a unique appearance to a garden.

Raised beds are convenient for those in wheelchairs and for those who cannot bend. The ideal height should be at least 2 feet, and not wider than 2 feet if it is against a wall, and not wider than 4 feet if it is worked from both sides. A path at least 3 feet wide should be laid on each side of the bed so that a wheelchair can be easily turned around.

The walls of a raised bed may be of masonry, of redwood or cypress sections, or of railroad ties. Masonry walls must be secured to concrete footings that are set in the ground at least 12 inches. Wooden walls should be stabilized by bolting to concrete blocks. A temporary bed can be made with peat blocks, but these tend to dry out fast and are not stable. A bed can easily be constructed by using paving slabs (36 by 24 by 2 inches) that are sunk 12 inches deep with 24 inches above the ground. Use gravel or rocks inside to stabilize the slabs. Place 12 to 15 inches of gravel and stone for drainage and the rest soil. The type of soil used depends on the plants growing in the raised bed. Initially, fill the bed to the top of the walls or even slightly higher. Let the soil settle for about a week, and then add enough soil so that the surface is 1/2 inch from the top of the walls. Have the soil tested periodically, and fertilize if necessary. With raised beds, care must be taken to prevent pressure from the soil overturning the retaining wall. Also, the problem of frost heaves under the wall can be minimized by good drainage that extends below the frost line.

Select plants that do not have extensive root systems. Most flowers, herbs, smaller vegetables, roses, and small shrubs can be grown in raised beds.

References

Sabel, M. 1967. "Red cross raised garden for the elderly, infirm and disabled. *J. Roy. Hort. Soc.* 92(12): 526-527.

Sunset Editors. 1969. *Garden and Patio Building Book.* Lane Books, Menlo Park, Ca.

GARDENING UNDER LIGHTS

Growing plants under fluorescent lights opens up a whole new world of gardening. Any type of plant, seed or cutting can be grown. It is easy, fun, and efficient.

Fluorescent Lights

Plants absorb principally from the blue and red ends of the solar spectrum at various stages of their life cycle (germination, growth, flowering, dormancy). They need the violet/blue end of the spectrum for growth, and the red/infrared end for flowering. Photosynthesis is more efficient when the fluorescent lights have the proper amounts of blue and red.

Incandescent lights (mostly red light) can be combined with ordinary fluorescent lights (mostly blue light) to grow plants. However, the incandescents give off too much heat and too little light for their wattage. There are many commercial fluorescent tubes available. These include Cool White or Deluxe Cool White tubes, Gro-Lux®, Gro-Lux Wide Spectrum®, Vitalite®, Agro-lite®, Tru-Bloom®, and Natur-escent®. Plants can be grown under a combination of one Cool White and one Warm White tube. Caution: never try to grow plants under a sunlamp!

The fluorescent tubes are mounted in fixtures that come in 2, 4 and 8 foot lengths. Most fixtures hold two or four tubes. There are also commercial fixtures equipped with legs, but standard industrial fixtures can be mounted or suspended with chains. Most industrial fixtures come with reflectors that concentrate the light onto the plants and not into the room. A two-tube fixture will provide adequate light for most plants in an area 1 foot in depth by the length of the fixture and tube. The tubes must be changed every eight months to a year.

Growing Under Lights

In general, the lights should be on fourteen to sixteen hours a day. Plants need a period of darkness to rest, with the exception of seeds and cuttings which may be grown under twenty-four hours of light until the seeds have germinated or the cuttings have rooted. For flowering plants, the photoperiod is very important. It is not always the light intensity and temperature that determine flowering, but the duration of night or darkness. Fall, winter, and spring blooming plants such as chrysanthemums, poinsettias, orchids, and Christmas cactus will bloom only if given long nights of fourteen to sixteen hours, or lights on eight to ten hours a day. Summer blooming plants including vegetables need eighteen hours of light and six hours of darkness. Geraniums, annuals, and seedlings of most plants fall into this category. Gesneriads (African violets and gloxinias), oxalis, and begonias are night neutral, and will bloom with six to eight hours of darkness or with the lights on fourteen to sixteen hours. Foliage plants not raised for bloom can have varying amounts of light and darkness. A timer can be used to turn the lights on and off when desired.

On the average, most plants are placed from 6 to 12 inches from the tubes. However, geraniums, annuals, and sun-loving plants should be as close to the lights as possible and as near to the middle of the tube as possible (there is less light intensity near the ends of the tubes). Seeds and cuttings should be placed 3 inches from the tubes. In general, observe the reactions of the plants. If they grow spindly, move them closer to the lights. If they turn yellow and the leaves curl under or are stunted, move them away from the lights. Remember that successful plant growth will depend not only on proper light but also on other factors such as water, proper soil, food, temperature, humidity, ventilation, and pest control.

Suggested Projects

Start seeds and cuttings under fluorescent lights.

Start annuals for the garden in March, perennials in June, houseplants and softwood cuttings of shrubs in midsummer, and hardwood cuttings in the fall.

Terrariums, dish gardens, and herbs grow well under lights. Various bulbs can be forced and grown under lights.

Attach fluorescent lights to tiered benches, old book cases, or under stairs. Set the plants on trays of moist gravel.

Tomatoes can be grown under lights if the temperature is maintained at 70-75° F and given sixteen hours of light. The cherry tomato *Tiny Tim* may be cultivated the year round under lights. Use Blossom-set® to initiate fruit set.

References

Cherry, E. C. 1965. *Fluorescent Light Gardening*. Van Nostrand Reinhold Co., New York

Elbert, G. A. 1973. *The Indoor Light Gardening Book*. Crown Publishers, Inc., New York

Kramer, J. 1974. *Plants Under Lights*. Simon & Schuster, New York

Krantz, F. H. and L. Jacqueline. 1971. *Gardening Indoors Under Lights*. Viking Press, New York

McDonald, E. 1965. *Complete Book of Gardening Under Lights*. Doubleday & Co., Inc., New York

GARDENS FOR THE BLIND

A garden where the visually handicapped can touch and "see" different kinds of plants opens up a new world for the blind. It helps to increase their enjoyment of plants and nature. The garden should not be isolated or separated from other areas. Both the sighted and the blind should be able to make use of it. The garden should be thought of as an area of selected plants that appeal not only to the sense of sight, but to the other senses as well.

A project to develop a garden can begin by contacting a local service club or other organizations concerned with the disabled. A public park or a local arboretum is a potential site, and they may be able to offer assistance in the project.

Choose an area that offers a variety of interesting natural features such as slopes, running brooks, and waterfalls. The garden may be in the shape of a loop or it may be circular. The garden should be self-guiding. Guideropes or metal rails that are 30 inches high are suggested. Ropes can be run through posts that are set 15 to 20 feet apart. At various stations, plaques are placed ,describing the plants in Braille or raised letters for the blind and in large type for others. The description should be short and simple, describing the plant's characteristics and where it is growing. The plaques should be 30 to 36 inches above the ground, and they should be slanted slightly forward. Raised beds can also be used, and benches can be provided for rest and meditation in the garden.

The plants may be arranged clockwise, including annuals and perennials in addition to trees and shrubs. Select varieties that appeal to the senses of touch and smell. People with visual handicaps are very interested in plants with strong textural characteristics (hairy, spines, thorns), in addition to fragrant flowers and foliage.

Selected Plants

For fragrance: beebalm, candytuft, Chinese witch hazel, chrysanthemums, daphne, evening primrose, freesia, hemlock, honeysuckle, iris, lemon daylily, lilac, lily-of-the-valley, marigolds, mock orange, peony, petunias, pines, pinks, roses, scented geraniums, snapdragons, stock, summer sweet, sweet alyssum, sweet autumn clematis, sweet pea, sweet shrub, various herbs, violets

For texture: azalea, barberry, cacti, English ivy, ferns, geraniums, grasses, holly, ironwood, lily, moss, pachysandra, poppies, rhododendrons, succulents, winged euonymus, zinnia.

References

Anonymous. 1972. "Blind visitors enjoy garden." *Sou. Flor. & Nur.* 85(18):52.
———. 1974. "Gardens for the blind: construction of a garden for the blind and handicapped at the Woodbridge, New Jersey Public Library." *Am. Lib.* 5: 409.
Collins, J. 1968. "The Braille Trail." *Trends in Parks and Rec.* 5(2): 1-3.
Honey, T. E. 1968. "Garden for the blind." *Home Gard. & Flow. Gro.* 55: 34-35.

Mihan, P. E. 1972. "Suggestions on building a garden for the visually handicapped." *Arbor. & Bot. Gard. Bul.* 6(3): 91-94.

Spinelli, A. J. and J. E. Earley. 1972. "Dual nature trails use both Braille and printed markers for use of visually handicapped campers." *Camp. Mag.* 44: 19.

Stevens, L. 1971. "Gardening without sight." *J. Roy. Hort. Soc. 96(5): 230-231.*

Wilson, H. V. P. and L. Bell. 1967. The Fragrant Year: Scented Plants for Your Garden and Your Home. M. Barrows & Co., Inc., New York

Gardens for the Blind in the United States

Helen Keller Fragrance Garden
Alabama School for the Deaf and Blind
Talladega, Alabama 35160

Mrs. W. R. Pinkerton*
5920 East Rosewood
Tucson, Arizona 85702

Chigo National Forest
2957 Birch Street
Bishop, California 93514

Muir Woods National Monument
Mill Valley, California 94941

Whispering Pines Braille Trail
U.S. Forest Service
San Bernardino National Forest
San Bernardino, California 92402

Strybling Arboretum
Golden Gate Park
9th Avenue & Lincoln Way
San Francisco, California 94101

Mrs. J. D. Sawir*
9525 West 71st Avenue
Arvada, Colorado 80002

Roaring Fork Braille Trail
White River National Forest
Aspen, Colorado 81611

Appalachicola National Forest
214 South Bronough Street
P.O. Box 1050
Tallahassee, Florida 32302

Fernbank Science Center
156 Heaton Park Drive N.E.
Atlanta, Georgia 30301

Georgia Academy for the Blind
Macon, Georgia 31208

Sunlight House
Massachusetts Association for the Blind
120 Boylston Street
Boston, Massachusetts 02181

School for the Deaf and Blind
Great Falls, Montana 59401

Shoal Harbor Marine Museum
Old Spy House
Port Monmouth Road
Port Monmouth, New Jersey 07758

Bergen County Wildlife Center
Wyckoff, New Jersey 07481

Mrs. E. Schifani
4819 Rayene N.E.
Albuquerque, New Mexico 87101

"La Pasada Encantada"
Sleepy Grass Campground
Lincoln National Forest
Cloudcroft, New Mexico 88317

---

*In charge of correspondence

Cienega Nature Trail for the Handicapped
Cibola National Forest
Sandia Crest, New Mexico 87047

Brooklyn Botanic Garden
1000 Washington Avenue
Brooklyn, New York 11225

Jewish Braille Institute of America
110 East 30th Street
New York, New York 10001

Asheville-Biltmore Botanical Garden
University of North Carolina at Asheville
Asheville, North Carolina 28804

"Feel of the Forest" Braille Trail
Hamilton County Park District
10245 Winton Road
Cincinnati, Ohio 45201

Longwood Gardens
Kennet Square, Pennsylvania 19348

John J. Tyler Arboretum
Lima, Pennsylvania 19060

Oerwood Nature Center
P.O. Box 461
Manchester, Pennsylvania 17345

Bureau of Conservation
Bozee Park
675 Oldfrankston Road
Pittsburgh, Pennsylvania 15230

Living Historical Gardens
Horticulture Department
Clemson University
Clemson, South Carolina 29631

Tennessee Botanical Gardens
Cheekwood
Nashville, Tennessee 37202

Fort Worth Botanic Gardens
3220 Botanic Garden Drive
Fort Worth, Texas 77001

U.S. Forest Service
Provo, Utah 84601

"Discovery Way"
Massanutten Mountain
George Washington National Forest
New Market, Virginia 22844

Norfolk Botanic Garden
Airport Boulevard
Norfolk, Virginia 23501

GRAFTING CACTI

This activity requires skill and practice. The technique can be used to create plant oddities with fascinating growth forms. A round or rippled cactus can be joined to a straight or columnar cactus, and many other combinations are possible.

Success depends upon joining the cut surfaces of a scion (a portion of a plant to be grafted) to a stock plant so that the growth layer (cambium) of both parts will be in contact with each other. The best time to graft cacti is during the growing season from May to October. The grafting stock must be healthy and vigorous, and the scion should be taken from fresh growing tips or new offshoots.

There are three methods that can be used:

1. *Flat graft:* This is the easiest. Select a stock plant and

make a flat, transverse cut with a clean, sharp knife. Treat the scion in the same way. Trim the edges to remove any loose tissue. Press the two flat surfaces together. Use pins, toothpicks, or rubber bands to hold the two pieces together. This method is suggested for round cacti.

2. *Cleft graft:* This involves fitting a *v*-cut scion into a wedge-shaped base. Secure the two pieces together. This method is recommended for flat scions.

3. *Side graft:* Both plants are cut on a slant, and the pieces are joined and secured. This method is recommended for slender scions.

Try to keep the open cuts as clean as possible. Place the grafted plants in the shade for a few days, and do not water or mist them. Check occasionally on the condition of the union, and loosen the rubber bands if necessary.

Some succulents in the *Euphorbia* family may also be grafted.

References

Cutak, L. 1956. *Cactus Guide.* D. Van Nostrand Co., Inc., New York
Sunset Editors. 1970. *Succulents and Cactus.* Lane Pub. Co., Menlo Park, Ca.

GROWING HERBS

Herbs are plants whose leaves, flowers, seeds, stems, and roots contain volatile oils. They include perennials, biennials, and annuals. Many herbs are both decorative and fragrant and may be grown indoors as houseplants, or outdoors in regular flower beds. If space is a problem, herbs can also be grown in pots and in other containers.

Many of the aromatic herbs originate from the Mediterranean region and are accustomed to growing in a warm, sunny location with a well-drained soil. Thyme, marjoram, basil, rosemary, winter savory, and sage like a warm, dry location and tend to develop more flowers and scent when grown in a somewhat poor soil. Parsley, chervil, lovage, balm, mint, and tarragon grow best in semishade.

Ideally, the herb garden should be sunny, face south or east, and have some shady areas. The herbs may be arranged in flower beds, borders, rock gardens, or in small formal herb gardens. Most designs use defined shapes such as squares, oblongs, triangles, circles, and ovals with paths leading through them. For the disabled, try to design the garden so that the plants can be easily reached with wide paths between rows or small groups of plants.

Most herbs are grown from seed. Some plants such as sage, lemon balm, and rosemary can easily be propagated from cuttings. Thyme and marjoram can be propagated by surface layering, chives and tarragon by division, and the mints by dividing the underground runners. For best results, start new plants in the fall by means of cuttings, or by crowns or root divisions.

The seeds may be sown anytime indoors for "kitchen gardening." Most of the herbs take two to three months to mature. For outdoor planting, start perennials indoors in late February and annuals in late March. Seeds may also be sown directly outdoors in the spring. Try not to cover the seeds too deeply.

Growing herbs in containers is a simple procedure. The containers may be clay pots, wooden planters, hanging baskets, or strawberry jars. The containers must have proper drainage. They should have three to five hours of direct sunlight, or the plants can also be grown under artificial lights. Water when thoroughly dry, and mist, pinch, and prune occasionally.

Suggested Projects

Plant herbs in a strawberry pot that has six, eight, or ten openings, each with a different herb.

Use various herbs for tea: one teaspoon of dried leaves or flowers is used for one cup of tea. If fresh herbs are used, double the amount, and steep in boiling water for ten to fifteen minutes.

Grow herbs in tubs and in window boxes.

Try making bonsai with oregano and sage plants.

Dry various herbs for potpourri.

Design a fragrance and texture garden for the blind.

Sink concrete blocks (cinder blocks) in the soil, and plant herbs inside the spaces.

References

Doole, L. E. 1973. *Herb Magic and Garden Craft.* Sterling Pub. Co., Inc., New York

Elbert, V. F. and G. A. Elbert. 1974. *Fun with Growing Herbs Indoors.* Crown Pubs. Inc., New York

Foster, G. B. 1973. *Herbs for Every Garden.* E. P. Dutton and Co., Inc., New York

Sunset Editors. 1974. *How to Grow Herbs.* Lane Books, Menlo Park, California

A List of Herbs

ambrosia *(Artemisia annua)*: annual, grows to 6 feet, feathery plumes of very aromatic, bright green foliage, sun

angelica *(Angelica archangelica)*: biennial, grows to 6 feet, very decorative, used in potpourri, semishade

anise *(Pimpinella anisum)*: annual, 2 feet, seeds used for flavoring, sun

balm "lemon" *(Melissa officinalis)*: perennial, 2 feet, shiny, dark green, heart-shaped foliage, very aromatic, sun or shade

basil sweet *(Ocimum basilicum)*: annual, 2 1/2 feet, bright green, fragrant leaves, sun

dwarf sweet *(O. minimum)*: annual, 9 inches, smaller leaves, sun

purple *(O. basilicum purpureum)*: annual, 2 1/2 feet, sweet, purple leaves, sun

dwarf purple *(O. minimum purpureum)*: annual, 9 inches, smaller leaves, sun

holy *(O. sanctum)*: annual, 2 feet, hairy, anise fragrance, sun

lemon *(O. basilicum citriodorus)*: annual, 2 feet, lemon fragrance, sun

curly *(O. crispum)*: annual 2 feet, bright green curly foliage, sun

beebalm *(Monarda didyma)*: perennial, aromatic foliage and bright red flowers, sun or semishade

borage *(Borago officinalis)*: annual, 3 feet, grey green, hairy, cucumber-flavored foliage, blue flowers, sun or semishade

caraway *(Carum carvi)*: biennial, 2 feet, lacy foliage, sun

catnip *(Nepeta cataria)*: perennial, 3 feet, grey green foliage, sun or shade

chamomile *(Anthemis nobilis)*: perennial, 3 to 12 inches, bright green leaves and daisylike flowers, good ground covers in semishade

chervil *(Anthriscus cerefolium)*: annual, 1 foot, fernlike anise-flavored leaves, semishade

chives *(Allium schoenoprasum)*: perennial, 18 inches, grasslike onion-flavored leaves, sun

clary *(Salvia sclarea)*: biennial, 3 feet, hairy foliage and spikes of lavender pink flowers, sun

coriander *(Coriandrum sativum)*: annual, 1 foot, lacy foliage, seeds used for flavoring, sun

costmary *(Chrysanthemum balsamita)*: perennial, 3 feet, bright green leaves, sun or semishade

dill *(Anethum graveolens)*: annual, 3 feet, feathery foliage, sun

fennel *(Foeniculum vulgare)*: perennial, 5 feet, feathery foliage, sun

feverfew *(Chrysanthemum parthenium)*: perennial, 1 to 3 feet, sun or semishade

garlic *(Allium sativum)*: perennial, 2 to 3 feet, sun

geraniums (*Pelargonium* species): perennials, 4 feet, leaves used in potpourri, sun to semishade

Rose *(P. graveolens)*: hairy, deep green lobed leaves

Lemon-scented *(P. crispum)*

Peach *(P. crispum* 'variegatum')

Lime *(P. nervosum)*

Nutmeg *(P. fragrans)*

Apple *(P. odoratissimum)*

Peppermint *(P. tomentosum)*

Apricot *(P. scabrum* 'M.Ninon')

Coconut *(P. giossularioides)*

horehound *(Marrubium vulgare)*: 18 inches, downy leaves and stems, sun

horseradish *(Armoracia rusticana)*: perennial, 2 feet, sun

hyssop *(Hyssopus officinalis)*: perennial, 18 inches, shrubby, dark green, narrow leaves, blue, white, or pink flowers, sun

lavender *(Lavandula vera)*: perennial, 1 foot, grey green aromatic foliage and lavender flowers, sun

lavender cotton *(Santolina chamaecyparissus)*: perennial, 1 foot, grey green foliage, sun

lavender cotton, green *(S. virens)*: perennial, 1 foot, bright emerald green foliage, sun

lemon verbena *(Aloysia triphylla)*: perennial, but nonhardy shrub, 4 feet, bright green foliage with lemon fragrance, sun

lovage *(Levisticum officinale)*: perennial, 5 feet, resembles celery in flavor and appearance, sun

marjoram *(Majorana hortensis)*: perennial, 1 to 2 feet, small, oval leaves, sun

mint apple *(Mentha rotundifolia)*: perennial, 3 feet, wooly foliage, sun

corsican *(M. requieni)*: moss like, very pungent, semishade

orange *(M. citratra)*: 2 feet, dark green leaves edged with purple, sun

spearmint *(M. spicata)*: 18 inches, bright green foliage, sun

nasturtium (*Tropaeolum* spp.): perennial grown as annual, 15 inches, peppery flavor, sun

oregano *(Origanum vulgare)*: perennial, 1 to 2 feet, light green foliage, sun

orris *(Iris florentina)*: perennial, 2 feet, pale lavender flowers, sun

our lady's bedstraw *(Galium verum)*: perennial, 18 inches, feathery, bright green leaves, fragrant yellow flowers, sun

parsley *(Petroselinum crispum)*: biennial, 9 inches, sun

rampion *(Campanula rapunculus)*: biennial, 2 feet, root used for flavoring, sun

rosemary *(Rosmarinus officinalis)*: perennial, but not hardy, 5 feet, needlelike, dark green foliage, sun

sage *(Salvia officinalis)*: perennial subshrub, 3 feet, gray, pungent leaves, sun pineapple *(S. rutilans)*: 4 feet, light green fuzzy foliage, sun

sesame *(Sesamum orientale)*: annual, 2 feet, sun

southernwood *(Artemisia abrotanum)*: perennial, 3 to 5 feet, lemon scent, sun

summer savory *(Satureja hortensis)*: annual, 18 inches, fragrant leaves, sun

sweet bay *(Laurus nobilis)*: perennial but not hardy, leathery leaves, sun

sweet cicely *(Myrrhis odorata)*: perennial, 2 feet, fernlike, licorice-flavored foliage, sun or semishade

sweet woodruff *(Asperula odorata)*: perennial, 9 inches, dark green foliage, sun

tansy *(Tanacetum vulgare)*: perennial, 4 feet, fernlike foliage and yellow flowers, sun or semishade

tarragon *(Artemisia dracunculus)*: perennial, 2 feet, dark green leaves, sun

thyme *(Thymus vulgaris)*: perennial, 1 foot, small subshrub, tiny grey green leaves, sun

creeping *(T. serpyllum)*: low growing, sun

lemon *(T. serpyllum citriodorus)*: low growing, sun

silver *(T. vulgaris argenteus)*: 9 inches, silvery, fragrant foliage, sun

winter savory *(Satureja montana):* perennial, 1 foot, dark green leaves, sun

wormwood *(Artemisia absinthium)*: 3 feet, grey green feathery foliage, sun

HANGING BASKETS

Hanging baskets utilize space which is not used for other purposes. By being suspended in the air and trailing in space, a leaf color may appear more vivid, translucent, and even iridescent. Hanging baskets can contribute to a feeling of serenity and give loftiness to a room, garden, terrace, or balcony.

Containers for hanging baskets may be made of plastic, clay, acrylic, glass, wood, or wire. Ordinary flower pots may be suspended with metal or macrame hangers. Special pottery jars with a number of side openings through which small plants may be inserted are sold commercially. Plastic fish bowls, old wire bird cages, lava or feather rock, a coconut shell cut in half, plastic sherbet and margarine tubs, and even plastic bags can be used for hanging baskets. Wire baskets can be constructed with the aid of pliers and a soldering iron, making sure that the spaces are not over one inch, and that the wire is securely held in place. A basket can also be made with wire mesh or chicken wire shaped and nailed to a piece of wood as a bottom board, and lined with moist peat moss.

A peat moss liner for wire baskets should be about 1 inch thick to keep the soil mixture from leaking through. First soak the moss in warm water, and then apply it to the wire basket. You can also use moss collected off rocks in the woods, but it must be peeled off in a solid, yet thin mat. The green surface is placed outward. Spanish moss is another material that makes an attractive liner.

A suitable growing medium consists of one part peat moss, one part potting soil, and one part perlite. The mixture is porous, light, and yet retains water. Synthetic soilless mixes may also be used. Make sure that there is proper drainage for adequate root aeration. Add 1 to 1 1/2 inches of drainage material in the bottom of plastic and clay hanging pots. Milled sphagnum moss may be used in combination with perlite, or just perlite alone for drainage. Wire baskets lined with sphagnum moss and wooden containers need no drainage material, and these are recommended for outdoor use.

To plant a wire basket, line the basket with moss, and then fill the lower half of the basket with soil. Those plants that are to grow laterally out of the basket are planted first. Each root ball is placed flat on it its side, and the plants are carefully pushed between the wires. Moss is placed between the root ball and the basket and around the crown of the plant. Plant the upright plants last, and fill the basket to the rim with soil.

Overwatering is a problem with most potted houseplants, but with hanging baskets, underwatering is the main problem. Water the basket by submerging it in water almost to its rim. When the soil is thoroughly saturated, hang it up to drain.

Frequent fertilizing is needed because more of the nutrients are leached away. Hanging baskets that are properly cared for usually grow faster than potted plants due to increased air circulation around the root systems, allowing for a larger water and nutrient uptake. Sphagnum moss thoroughly moistened with a weak solution of complete fertilizer may also be used in place of soil. The basket is dipped once a week in the same weak fertilizer solution.

Suggested Plants

asparagus fern (*A. densiflorus* 'Sprengeri')
baby tears *(Helxine soleirolii)*
brazil oxalis *(Oxalis braziliensis)*
bronze wandering Jew *(Zebrina purpusii)*
burro's tail *(Sedum morganianum)*
creeping charlie *(Plectranthus australis)*
English ivy *(Hedera helix)*
flame violet (*Episcia* spp.)
fuchsia begonia *(Begonia fuchsioides)*
German ivy *(Senecio mikanioides)*
giant white inch plant (*Tradescantia albiflora* 'Albo-vittata')
golden pothos *(Scindapsus aureus)*
grape ivy *(Cissus rhombifolia)*
heartleaf philodendron *(P. oxycardium)*
impatiens *(I. walleriana sultanii)*
ivy geranium *(Pelargonium peltatum)*
lipstick plant *(Aeschynanthus lobbianus)*
lovely browallia *(B. speciosa major)*
mother of thousands *(Saxifraga sarmentosa)*
petunia *(Petunia* spp.)
piggyback plant *(Tolmiea menziesii)*
prayer plant *(Maranta leuconeura)*
purple passion vine *(Gynura sarmentosa)*
purple wandering Jew *(Zebrina pendula)*
rosary vine *(Ceropegia woodii)*
spider plant (*Chlorophytum* spp.)
strawberry begonia *(Saxifraga sarmentosa)*

Swedish ivy *(Plectranthus australis)*
Tahitian bridal veil *(Gibasis geniculata)*
trailing lobelia *(L. erinus)*
tricolor wandering Jew (*Z. pendula* 'Discolor')
wax plant (*Hoya* spp.)

In addition, try various herbs, strawberries, sweet potatoes, dwarf cucumbers, mini-tomatoes, creeping junipers, vinca, and training evergreens.

References

Coleman, M. J. (ed.). 1975. *Hanging Plants for Modern Living.* Merchants Pub. Co., Kalamazoo, Mich.

Kramer, J. 1971. *Hanging Gardens.* Charles Scribner's Sons, New York

Mabe, R. E. 1973. *Gardening in Hanging Baskets.* Potpourri Press, Greensboro, N.C.

Sunset Editors. 1974. *Hanging Gardens.* Lane Books, Menlo Park, Ca.

HYDROPONIC GARDENING

This is a simple and interesting activity. The root development is fascinating to observe, and there are no worries about overwatering, underwatering, or soil diseases. Various house plants can be easily grown in nutrient solutions.

Any container can be used except for copper, brass, or lead which tend to react with water and fertilizers. Flasks, beakers, test tubes, antique jars and bottles, and hyacinth glasses can be used.

Most plants need no support other than the sides of the container. Some plants need support until they develop roots. Use aquarium gravel, sea glass, broken crockery, stones, pebbles, and colored marbles. Florist's oasis can be used for cuttings and flowers.

Cleanliness is very important. All containers must be cleaned at least once a month, and the roots and stems should be rinsed and wiped off. Bottle brushes are useful for cleaning. Avoid tap water that is treated with chlorine or water softened with chemicals. The pH should be between 6 and 7. Rain water is satisfactory. The nutrient solution can be made with any plant food, but cut the dosage in half. A suitable solution is made with one teaspoon of 20-20-20 per gallon of water. Place a few pieces of charcoal on the bottom of the container to keep the water fresh. Initially, add plain water to cover the roots and part of the stem of the plants. Do not let any leaves remain submerged or they will rot. After a few days, replace the plain water with the nutrient solution. When the nutrient solution evaporates, always add *plain* water. Watch for algae and dead roots. Change the solution at least once a month. Aquarium pumps can be used to aerate the water from time to time.

Suggested plants

Arrowhead *(Syngonium)*, bloodleaf *(Iresine)*, Chinese evergreens *(Aglaonema)*, *Coleus*, *Dracaena*, dumb cane *(Dieffenbachia)*, English ivy *(Hedera)*, *Forsythia*, German ivy *(Senecio)*, miracle plant *(Fatshedera)*, oleander *(Nerium)*, *Pachysandra*, periwinkle, *Philodendron*, piggy-back plant *(Tolmiea)*, pothos, *(Scindapsus)*, pussy willows *(Salix)*, spiderworts *(Tradescantia)*, Swedish ivy *(Plectranthus)*, sweet flag *(Acorus)*, sweet potato *(Ipomoea)*, umbrella plant *(Cyperus)*, wandering jew *(Zebrina)*

Suggested Projects

Forcing Bulbs in Water

Hyacinths: Fill a container with water so that it just touches the bottom of the bulb, and place it in the refrigerator. Leave it for a month, and check the water and root development. The bulb must have sufficient roots to bloom. When roots have filled the container, remove it from the refrigerator, and place it in a cool, shady area for five days. Then bring it to a cool, sunny area. Start the bulbs in November to have blooms by December.

Crocus: Use gravel or sand, and make sure that the bulbs are always out of the water. Follow the refrigerator routine, and remove them after the roots have developed.

Narcissus (Paper-whites): Use gravel to support the bulbs. Place them in a cool (50-60° F), dark, well-ventilated area until the shoots are three inches tall. Move them to a north window for three to four days, and then place them in the sun.

Lily-of-the-valley: Place the pips in gravel or sand with the buds just above the surface. Water thoroughly and place them in a cardboard box with holes for two weeks at room temperature. Then, gradually expose them to more light.

A MINI-INDOOR REFLECTING POOL

Use a traylike container made of plastic or plexiglass that holds 2 to 3 inches of water. Set this on a platform of bricks or wooden blocks, 12 inches above the floor. Line the outside of the container with cork bark, moss, or other decorative material. Set the plants on needle holders raised on stones so that only the roots are submerged. Cover the roots and holder with gravel and moss. Use charcoal in the water, and change the water every ten to fourteen days. Place a light on the floor so that it shines through the bottom.

References

Bridwell, R. 1972. *Hydroponic Gardening: The Magic of Hydroponics for the Home Gardener.* Woodbridge Press Pub. Co., Santa Barbara, Ca.

Douglas, J. S. 1972. *Beginner's Guide to Hydroponics.* Drake Publishers, Inc., New York

Loewer, H. P. 1974. *The Indoor Water Gardener's How To Handbook.* Popular Lib. Inc., New York

KITCHEN GARDENING

Many fruits and vegetables that are used in the kitchen are potential sources for house plants. They are easy to grow, and the seeds are readily available. These plants are interesting and fun for children, and they cost next to nothing.

Avocado (Persea americana and P. drynifolia)

Soak the pit in warm water for four to five days. Peel off the brown skin that covers the pit and cover two thirds of the pit with soil (the pit may also be started in water, but it takes longer, and the pit tends to rot). Make sure that the larger, flattened and slightly indented end is downward. Germination takes four to five weeks and occurs best at 80-85° F, but it will also germinate at room temperature. Pinch back the top when the plant is 6 inches tall to encourage branching. They require full sun.

Birdseed

Try germinating the seeds on moist cotton or cheese cloth. Some commercial brands, however, are specially treated, and the seeds will not grow.

Carrots

Cut off the top inch of the carrot, and place it in a bowl of moist sand or gravel. Set it in a sunny location. Lush green leaves will emerge. Other plants with tap roots such as beets and turnips can also be grown in this way.

Citrus

Use grapefruit, lemon, lime, orange, and tangerine seeds. Place the seed in ½ inch of soil, and place in a warm location (70° F). The plants have dark green, shiny foliage. Give full sun.

Coconut

Germination takes about two months, and the husk must be attached. Partially plant it in moist sand at a slight angle with the depression end upward. Mist this end everyday.

Coffee

Use green or unroasted beans. Germination takes about two months. Foliage is a waxy green. Give full sun.

Dates

Obtain unpasteurized dates from a health food store. Soak them in water for a week, and cover with 1 inch of soil. Foliage is feathery. Give full sun.

Grapes

Sow the seeds in the soil. Train the vines, and give full sun.

Onions

Place the bottom end of the onion in water. Keep it in the dark until roots appear. Then, move it to a sunny window. A flower sometimes forms.

Pineapple

Cut the top of the fruit off, and let it dry for a day before planting it in moist, acid soil (add coffee grounds).

Pomegranate (Punica granatum)

Sow the seeds 1/2 inch deep in moist soil. Germination takes six to eight weeks.

Sugar cane (Saccharum officinarum)

Propagate by cutting the stem into sections with each section having a node. Plant these in moist soil. Some will need a cold treatment before they grow.

Sweet Potato

Do not use oven-dried or those treated with growth inhibitors. Put the bottom half of the potato in water and place in the dark. Roots develop in ten to fourteen days. Remove most of the new shoots, leaving three or four shoots. Plant in soil and train the vines to grow around a sunny window.

White Potato

Cut the potato into sections with each section having two or three eyes or buds. Cover with three inches of soil. Place in a sunny window.

References

Kramer, J. 1975. *Kitchen Garden Book.* Bantam Books, Inc., Des Plaines, Ill.
Langer, R. W. 1971. *After Dinner Gardening Book.* The Macmillan Co., New York.
———. 1974. *The After-Dinner Gardening Book: The Avocado-Gift Edition.* The Macmillan Co., New York
Riemer, J. 1975. *The Beginner's Kitchen Garden Book.* Wm. Morrow & Co., Inc., West Caldwell, N.J.
Whitman, J. 19 6. *Starting from Scratch: A Guide to Indoor Gardening.* Quadrangle/The New York Times Book Co., Inc., New York

SAND PAINTING

Sand of various colors can be used to decorate the bottom of a closed terrarium or an open dish garden. Any clear glass or plastic container can be used to create a design of beauty.

Materials

Materials needed are containers, sand of various colors (Terrasand®), plastic spoons, a pointed tool about 12 inches long (a knitting needle or a pencil will do), gravel, potting soil.

Procedure

With a plastic spoon, place alternate layers of colored sand in a container until a sufficient height is reached. Use a dark color for the last or top layer so that any mixing with the soil will be less conspicuous. Place two inches of soil on top of these layers, and set in plants.

With practice, mound the layers of sand, and build them up so that various designs result. Use the point of the slender tool to make indentations so that the upper layer of sand will filter into the lower layer. Do not withdraw the tool directly upward, but move it backward a short distance so that a furrow is made, and then remove the tool. Add sand to hide these furrows and to level off the top layer. To conserve sand, place the potted plant into the container after the first layer of sand is added, and then build up layers around the pot.

Sometimes algae will form if it is too sunny and if water seeps through the soil into the layers of sand. This can be prevented by making the design around a flower pot and just watering the pot, or by pouring a layer of molten wax or placing a plastic lining over the design, letting it dry or settle, and then adding the soil or growing medium.

Cacti are very appropriate plants because they can grow in sand and require very little water.

References

Axelrod, H. R. 1975. *Sand Painting for Terrariums and Aquariums.* T. F. H. Publications, Inc., Neptune, N.J.
Miller, A. P. 1975. *Sand Design for Aquariums and Terrariums.* T. F. H. Publications, Inc., Neptune, N.J.

TERRARIUMS

A terrarium is a miniature garden growing in a covered container. It is a form of indoor gardening, but on a much smaller scale. It may be a desert terrarium that is dry and sunny, a marsh scene that is wet and humid, or a woodland environment that is cool and shady. A terrarium offers ideal growing conditions for plants. When properly maintained, it provides balanced light, temperature, water, and soil conditions. Moreover, it provides a high level of humidity, and diseases rarely enter this isolated garden. A terrarium can even be used for a seedling bed or a "plant hospital" for ailing plants.

For the disabled, this activity can be completed in a short time, and it is excellent exercise for the arms and fingers.

Materials

Use clear or light-colored containers. Those with wide openings are the easiest to plant in. It is difficult to get plants and soil into small-necked containers without tools. Use wide-mouthed jars such as gallon size mayonnaise, peanut butter, or pickle jars. Open globes, brandy snifters, fish bowls, aquarium tanks, glass canisters, display domes, decanters, antique fruit jars, goblets, medicine bottles, plastic containers, and plexiglass cubes can be used.

The growing medium should be one part sand, one part loam, and one part peat moss. Commercial African violet mixes are excellent for most plants. For a desert garden of cacti and succulents, use more sand and a small amount of bonemeal or superphosphate. For insectivorous plants, use pure sphagnum moss for the growing medium. The drainage material should be 1/8 to 1/4 inch deep for each inch of growing medium, and the depth of the medium should be 1/4 inch for each inch of the container's height. Crushed stone, pebbles, or perlite can be used for drainage. A thin layer (1/4-1/2 inch) of charcoal also aids in drainage, and it also helps to keep the soil sweet.

Tools can be made or bought. These include long bamboo sticks, a pick-up tool such as giant tweezers or mechanical fingers known as *astrofingers,* and scissors or shears. A tamper tool to firm the medium around the plants can be made by attaching a small cork to the end of a stick. For an insertion tool, a piece of wire 15 inches long with an opened loop on one end can be made from coat hangers. A metal or paper funnel, a sprayer, and a pruning tool are also suggested.

Accent materials such as lichens, pebbles, seashells, driftwood, small pocket mirrors for pools, and various ceramic figurines may be included in the garden.

Maintenance

Plants growing in a terrarium need sufficient light but never direct sunlight. The flowering and variegated plants need more light. A terrarium also grows well under artificial or fluorescent lights. The container should be turned from time to time for balanced growth. Prune the plants to prevent crowding and to permit sufficient light and air to reach the plants. The temperature should be 55-70° F.

Overwatering is the major cause for failure. Too much water encourages mold and spoilage. Add 1/4 cup of water to one gallon containers or less, and 1/2 cup to larger containers. Water the terrarium only if the soil feels dry 1/2 to 1 inch below the surface. If a faint mist shows on the sides of the container, there is adequate moisture. If there is excess condensation, remove the cover to permit ventilation and evaporation. A mold or gray fungus is the most common terrarium disease. To prevent this, spray the plants with a fungicide.

Planting the Terrarium

1. First add the drainage material, then a layer of charcoal, and then the soil. Use a funnel to direct the media into the container. A layer of sphagnum moss between the charcoal and soil will prevent the soil from sifting into the gravel.
2. Arrange the soil layer with a stick. Make slopes, hills, and terraces. Make a depression in the soil for the first plant.
3. Prepare the plants for insertion by making a ball or core around the roots by carefully rolling the root ball in paper towels. Place the looped wire around the collar of the plant, or use the pick-up tool if the opening is very narrow. Direct the plant's roots first into the container with the pick-up tool. Then, guide the leaves through carefully.
4. Position the plant, and set the roots about 1/2 inch deep. Apply pressure around the base of the plant with the

tamper tool. Place the tallest plants in first, then the smaller ones, and the ground covers last.

5. Tap the leaves with a stick or fine brush to remove any soil particles. Add any accent materials.
6. Water the terrarium by directing the flow of water down the sides of the container.
7. Cover the container and place it in diffuse light.
8. Check from time to time for water, pruning and diseases.

Suggested Plants

Select plants that prefer high humidity, moist soil, constant temperature, and a medium light intensity. The plants should be compatible with each other with respect to their growth requirements. Select plants that grow relatively slowly, and consider using miniature varieties. The plants in a terrarium should vary in height, shape, color of foliage, and in leaf forms. Usually a single plant is chosen as the dominant plant, and the others are arranged around it. For dry terrariums, use cacti and succulents. A list of recommended plants follows:

African violets (*Saintpaulia* spp. — miniature varieties)
artillery plant *(Pilea microphylla)*
asparagus ferns (*Asparagus* spp.)
baby tears *(Helxine soleirolii)*
balsam plant (*Impatiens* spp.)
begonias
bromeliads
caladiums (*Caladium humboldtii* — a miniature)
Chinese evergreens (*Aglaonema* spp.)
creeping charlie *(Plectranthus australis)*
cycads (*Zamia fischeri* — a dwarf)
English ivy *(Hedera helix)*
flame violets (*Episcia* spp.)
grape ivy (*Cissus striata* — a miniature)
irish moss (*Selaginella* spp.)
lichens, liverworts, and lycopods
Maidenhair ferns (*Adiantum* spp.)
mother of thousands *(Saxifraga sarmentosa)*

orchids (*Bulbophyllum barbigerum* — a miniature)
peperomias (*Peperomia* spp.)
prayer plant *(Maranta leuconeura)*
purple passion plant *(Gynura sarmentosa)*
snake plant (*Sansevieria* spp.)
spider plant (*Chlorophytum* spp.)
spider worts (*Tradescantia* spp.)
sundew *(Drosera rotundifolia)*
wandering Jews (*Zebrina* spp.)
woodland plants: ferns, moss, mushrooms, partridge berries, pipsissewa, rattlesnake plantain, snowberry, trailing arbutus, wild strawberry, wintergreen.

Additional Projects

Mini-terrariums: Clear plastic cups and glasses of various sizes can be inverted and used for mini-terrariums. Also, plant miniature plants in clear glass Christmas tree ornaments and in plastic containers from bubble gum and novelty machines.

A Partridge Berry Bowl: Fill an apothecary jar to the top with damp sphagnum moss. Insert red partridge berries and rattlesnake plantains toward the outside. Decorate with a red ribbon. Ideal around Christmas time.

Use carnivorous plants such as, Venus's flytrap, pitcher plants, and sundews for a children's program.

References

Ashberry, A. 1964. *Bottle Gardens and Fern Cases.* Bonanza Books, New York
Elbert, V. and G. A. Elbert. 1973. *Fun with Terrarium Gardening.* Crown Pub. Inc., New York
Fitch, C. M. 1974. *The Complete Book of Terrariums.* Hawthorne Books, Inc., New York
Grubman, B. J. 1973. *Introduction to Terrariums.* Popular Lib. Inc., New York
Kramer, J. 1969. *Gardens Under Glass: The Miniature Greenhouse in a Bottle, Bowl or Dish.* Simon & Schuster, Inc., New York
Mabe, R. E. 1973. *Gardening with Terrariums.* Greensboro, N.C.
Sunset Editors. 1973. *Terrariums and Miniature Gardens.* Lane Pub. Co., Menlo Park, Ca.

TOPIARY

This is the practice of pruning and shaping trees, shrubs, and other plants to obtain various shapes such as animals, houses, or geometric forms.

Plants such as boxwood, yew, and privet are commonly used. Plants such as ivies can be trained to cover wire forms. The preshaped wire form is placed around or under the plant, and the plant is trained to grow over the form by attaching it with wire or tape. Select plants that grow fast and that have numerous small leaves. Use variegated varieties with different leaf shapes and sizes. Philodendrons and creeping figs are ideal.

To make a more formal design, fill a wire-mesh form with damp sphagnum moss. Insert rooted cuttings into the moss, and secure them with nonrusting pins. Mist daily and fertilize every two weeks. Prune the new growth to shape the plant.

Suggested Projects

A hanging planter of any desired shape can be made by shaping wire mesh and filling it with moist sphagnum moss. Insert ferns, ivy, and epiphytes.

A plant totem pole can be made by shaping the wire mesh into a cylinder and filling it with sphagnum moss. Insert the plants through the sides of the cylinder.

Topiary Coleus: start with a rooted cutting, and remove side shoots so that heads or groups of leaves remain along the stem and/or at the top of the plant. Frequent pinching produces bushy, tight heads and keeps it in shape.

Herb trees: many of the woody, small-leaved herbs such as myrtle, rosemary, santolina, and thyme can be shaped by constant pruning and pinching into treelike forms. Occasional root pruning is also necessary to keep the roots and top growth in balance.

References

Hadfield, M. 1971. *Topiary and Ornamental Hedges.* St. Martin's Press, Inc.,

New York

Ishimoto, T. and K. Ishimoto. 1967. *Art of Shaping Shrubs, Trees and Other Plants.* Crown Pubs. Inc., New York

VEGETABLE GARDENING

A vegetable garden can be a source of pleasure and relaxation, a source of healthful exercise, and an educational experience for both children and adults.

Vegetables can be grown in pots, tubs, hanging baskets, window boxes, and, of course, in the ground. To grow successfully, vegetables need full sun, fertile soil, good drainage, a minimum of competition from roots of trees and shrubs, and an adequate supply of water.

Site Selection

1. The garden should receive a full day of sun. However, leafy crops will adapt to more shaded conditions.
2. Choose a level site. Avoid steep slopes and low spots. A southern slope is ideal.
3. Space is a limiting factor. Plan a small garden, for it stands less chance of being neglected. Locate the garden near a building, a water supply and the tools. The size of the garden will determine the tools needed. Even a mini-garden will require a hoe, rake, and spade or shovel. Larger gardens need more and larger equipment to make the project fun and easier to handle.

Planning the Garden

1. First obtain local information concerning the earliest and latest safe planting dates for vegetables, and any other special garden practices and varieties that are best for your area. One can obtain this information from state and county agricultural agents.
2. Plan the garden to scale on paper. If the garden is to be planted on sloping ground, plan to run the rows across the slope rather than up and down. This will reduce

runoff.

3. Arrange the garden so that tall plants such as corn or staked tomatoes are grouped together on one side of the garden. The north side of the garden is ideal.
4. Plant perennial crops on one side of the garden so that the remainder of the garden can be easily cultivated without disturbing them.
5. Group early-maturing crops together so that after harvest, the ground can be reworked, fertilized, and re-planted. This is called succession planting.
6. Space various plantings two to three weeks apart to provide a continuous supply of vegetables throughout the growing season.
7. If space is limited, avoid planting cucumbers, melons, or corn. Corn must be planted in blocks of three to four rows, and not in single, long rows. Employ the practice of interplanting: plant squash between corn or pole beans, or train pole beans to grow around corn stalks.
8. Practice crop rotation to prevent diseases that build up in the soil. Do not plant the same crop in the same place year after year.
9. Select crops that are time-tested, standard varieties that are resistant to disease and are easy to grow.
10. To save space, plant vine crops such as cucumbers, squash, and melons on the side of the garden, and let them spread into the fence row or yard.

Soil Preparation, pH, Fertilizing, Watering, Pest Control

Refer to Chapters Five and Six.

Starting Plants from Seeds, Transplanting, Setting in the Garden

Refer to Chapter Six and to the list of vegetables in this chapter.

Kinds of Vegetables to Grow

Early cool-weather crops: These can be planted as soon as the ground can be worked. They are also late fall crops.

beets, broccoli, cabbage, endive, kale, kolrabi, lettuce, onion sets, radishes, parsley, peas, spinach, turnips.

Mid-spring crops: These are planted after the last killing frost.

beans, beets, carrots, cauliflower, corn, onion sets, parsnips, potatoes, swiss chard, tomatoes.

Late spring — early summer crops: These are planted when soil and weather are warm.

cantaloupe, celery, eggplant, cucumber, lima beans, peppers, pumpkins, squash, watermelon

A Vegetable Garden Calender

This timetable of activities may be helpful. Make allowances for local weather conditions, and make adjustments for your area by back dating in southern areas or advancing in northern areas.

January: Look through seed catalogs and order the seeds. Plant onion seeds in the hotbed to be planted outdoors later. Start to plan the garden: row spacing, planting dates, succession plantings, and harvest times.

February: Plant cabbage, broccoli, and head lettuce in late February in a hotbed or indoors.

March: Transplant early started seedlings and keep them in the hotbed. Prepare flats for indoor sowing. Spread manure on the garden.

April: Start tomato, eggplant, and pepper seeds in flats or peat pots. If weather permits, till the soil. Plant early cabbage, broccoli, head lettuce, onion sets, peas, and other early season crops in late April. Start squash, melons, and cucumbers in peat pots in late April.

May: Most of the garden should be completely tilled. Set tomatoes out by the middle of the month, but if frost threatens, cover them with hot caps. Plant peppers, eggplant, potatoes, and beans. After hardening off the squash, melon, and cucumber seedlings, plant them outdoors in late May. Plant corn by the end of May. Harvest some of the early season crops, and reseed to continue the next succession.

June: Continue succession plantings of radishes and lettuce (heat-resistant varieties). Fertilize at the end of June.

July: Continue to weed, mulch, and harvest. Last chance to plant beans, spinach, kale, late turnips, late lettuce, cabbage, parsnips, and broccoli before frost arrives.

August: Plant fall maturing crops such as spinach, turnips, beets, radishes, and lettuce.

September: Order seed for green manure cover crop. Continue to harvest and clean up garden areas as they mature.

October: General garden cleanup. Mulch strawberry beds. Store root crops. Till areas and plant green manure cover crop.

November: Complete garden cleanup.

December: Order seed catalogs.

Suggested Projects

Plant a mini-garden (10 by 10 feet), and use midget varieties.

Plant vegetables in raised beds for those in wheelchairs and for those who cannot bend.

A raised mini-garden can be made in a large wooden tray supported by wooden supports.

Plant vegetables in window boxes and in containers.

Make use of vertical space by planting vines of beans, cucumbers, tomatoes, squash, and gourds near fences for support.

Make a vegetable tree by fastening concrete reinforcing wire to a backboard in the shape of a half-cylinder. Line the inside of the cylinder with black plastic, and fill it with synthetic growing medium. Slit the plastic in various places, and insert lettuce plants or a few tomato or cucumber plants.

A tomato ring can be made by making a circle 3 to 5 feet in

diameter with chicken wire or wire mesh, and filling the inside with 1 to 2 feet of compost, soil, and manure. The plants are placed equidistant around the outside of the circle, and they are attached to the wire with twine. Water the center of the circle so that nutrients will diffuse outward to the plants.

References

Carleton, R. M. 1967. *Vegetables for Today's Gardens.* D. Van Nostrand Co., Inc., Princeton, N.J.

Cook, C. (ed.). 1975. *Down-to-Earth Vegetable Gardening Know How.* Garden Way Pub. Co., Charlotte, Vt.

Faust, J. L. 1975. *The New York Times Book of Vegetable Gardening.* Quadrangle/The New York Times Book Co., New York

Fell, Dereck. 1975. *How to Plant a Vegetable Garden.* Barnes & Noble, Inc., Scranton, Pa.

Griffith, R. 1975. *Vegetable Garden Handbook: A Planning 4 Planting Record Book.* Garden Way Pub. Co., Charlotte, Vt.

Sunset Editors. 1973. *Guide to Organic Gardening.* Lane Books, menlo Park, Ca.

———. 1975. *Vegetable Gardening.* Lane Books, Menlo Park, Ca.

A List of Midget Varieties of Vegetables*

Beets: Baby Canning Beet No. 203 (Earl May) Detroit Dark Red (Burpee, Parks)

Cabbage: Earliana (Burpee), Baby Head Cabbage No. 231 (Earl May), Dwarf Modern (Parks)

Cantaloupe: Minnesota Midget (Parks), Early Sugar Midget No. 445 (Earl May), Burpee's Netted Gem (Burpee)

Carrots: Little Finger (Burpee), Tiny Sweet (Parks)

Corn: Golden Midget (Burpee, Parks), Midget Sweet No. 141 (Earl May), Midget Hybrid (Parks)

Cucumber: Cherokee (Parks), Patio Pik No. 366 (Earl May)

Egg plant: Morden Midget (Parks), Early Beauty Hybrid

---

*Sources:

W. Atlee Burpee Co. Philadelphia, P. 19132, Riverside, C. 92502, Clinton, Iowa 52732

Earl May Seed and Nursery Co., Shendoah, Iowa 51601

Geo. W. Park Seed Co. Inc., Greenwood, South Carolina 29646

Table III: Planting Details For Some Vegetables

	Depth to plant seeds	Distance between plants	Distance between rows	Days to Germination	Days to Maturity
Asparagus	½″	18″	36″	14	3 years
pole	1″	36″	30″	7-14	85-95
Bean, Lima					
bush	1″	3″	24″	7-14	70-80
pole	1″	36″	30″	7-14	60-70
Bean, Snap					
bush	1″	3″	24″	5-10	50-60
Beets	½″	3″	18″	7-12	55-60
Broccoli	¼″	24″	30″	6-9	70-80
Brussels sprouts	¼″	18″	3′	6-9	70-80
Cabbage	¼″	18″	24″	6-9	60-90
Carrots	¼″	3″	18″	12-18	60-75
Cauliflower	½″	18″	24″	6-9	60-80
Chard	½″	6″	24″	7-12	55-65
Collard	¼″	18″	30″	6-9	85-95
Corn, Sweet	½″	10″	36″	5-12	70-85
Cucumber	½″	48″ between hills	48″	7-10	65-70
Eggplant	½″	24″	36″	10-14	80-90
Endive	¼″	6″	18″	10-14	80-90
Kale	¼″	12″	18″	6-9	50-65
Kohlrabi	¼″	4″	24″	6-9	55-65
Lettuce, Head	¼″	8″-12″	18″	5-10	55-80
Lettuce, Leaf	¼″	3″	18″	5-10	35-50
Muskmelon	½″	60″ between hills	48″	7-12	80-90
Mustard Greens	¼″	3″	18″	5-8	35-45
Okra	½″	12″	30″	8-12	55-60
Seed	¼″	3″	18″	7-12	100-200
Onion					
Sets					25-35
Parsley	¼″	4″	24″	15-20	80-90
Parsnip	¼″	3″	24″	15-20	150
Peas	1″	2″	24″	7-10	60-75
Peppers	¼″	18″	30″	10-14	65-80
Potatoes	4″	12″	30″		100-120
Pumpkin	½″	60″ between hills	48″	7-12	110
Radish	¼″	1″	18″	3-6	25-35
Rhubarb	1″	30″	48″	12-20	2 years
Spinach	¼″	4″	18″	7-12	40-50
Squash, summer (bush)	½″	60″ between hills	48″	7-10	50-60
Squash, winter (vine)	½″	72″ between hills	48″	7-10	5-110
Sweet Potatoes		24″	30″		150
Tomato	½″	18″	48″	7-14	75-90
Turnip	¼″	6″	18″	5-10	40-60
Watermelon	½″	96″ between hills	96″	7-12	85-95

(Burpee)

Lettuce: Tom Thumb (Burpee, Parks), Midget No. 414 (Earl May)

Summer Squash: St. Pat Scallop (Burpee), Hybrid Zucchini (Burpee)

Tomatoes: Pixie Hybrid (Burpee), Tiny Tim (Burpee, Earl May, Parks), Pretty Patio (Earl May)

Watermelon: New Hampshire Midget (Burpee, Earl May), Lollipop (Parks), Sugar Baby (Parks, Burpee, Earl May)

A List of Giant Varieties of Vegetables*

Pumpkins: Big Max (up to 100 lbs.) (Earl May)

Tomatoes: Beefmaster (Parks) — up to 2 pounds

Delicious (Burpee) — over 1 pound

Cabbage: Hybrid O-S (Burpee, Earl May) — up to 20 pounds

Watermelon: Black Diamond (Parks, Earl May) — up to 125 pounds

WINDOW BOX GARDENING

Window boxes are used to cover bare walls, to emphasize objects, to blend a building with its surroundings, and to save space.

A window box can be made of redwood or cypress, plastic or metal. Yellow pine will last a long time if it is painted. All joints should be thoroughly painted before the box is put together, and brass screws should be used instead of nails. The minimum inner width should be 7 to 8 inches. This will allow ample space for two rows of plants, one of which may be an upright kind and the other a hanging type to cover the front of the box. The depth should be 7 to 8 inches. The most convenient length is 3 to 4 feet.

---

*Sources:

W. Atlee Burpee Co. Philadelphia, P. 19132, Riverside, C. 92502, Clinton, Iowa 52732

Earl May Seed and Nurserq Co., Shendoah, Iowa 51601

Geo. W. Park Seed Co. Inc., Greenwood, South Carolina 29646

Preparing the Box for Planting

1. Place a shard over each drainage hole. Then, cover these with a 1-inch layer of drainage material (gravel, pebbles, or perlite).
2. The soil must be rich, well drained, and yet retain moisture. A suitable mixture consists of three parts loam and one part well-rotted manure, leafmold, or peat moss.
3. When the plants are first placed in the box, they should be given a thorough watering to settle the soil. Always water until it begins to seep through the drainage holes.
4. Fertilize the plant every two weeks after the first month with liquid manure or a high-grade plant food. The soil should be renewed each year before planting.

Seeds may be started in a window box, but it is advisable to start them early in a hotbed or sow them in small clay or peat pots. Plants already potted are more desirable than those grown in flats or in the open ground because the root system is confined and less shock will result from transplanting.

Suggested Plants

FOR SUNNY LOCATIONS:

Flowers: ageratum, sweet alyssum, everblooming begonia, candytuft, geranium, heliotrope, lantana, lobelia, dwarf marigold, mignonette, mesembryanthemum, nasturtium, petunia

Foliage: acalypha, aspidistra, coleus, croton, dusty miller, golden feather, iresine, pandanus, sansevieria

Vines: asparagus ferns, English ivy, tuberous begonia, forget-me-not, fuchsia, German ivy, trailing geranium, trailing lantana, vinca, wandering Jew

FOR SHADY LOCATIONS:

Foliage: Boston fern, caladium, coleus, croton, maidenhair fern, Norfolk Island pine, Phoenix palm, rex begonia, san-

sevieria, umbrella plant
Vines: asparagus ferns, English ivy, German ivy, variegated
panicum, wandering jew

Suggested Combinations:

geraniums and English ivy with a palm in the center
petunias, vinca, asparagus and Boston ferns
Pink petunias and vinca
boxwood and rubber plants
screwpine, fancyleaf caladium, and dusty miller
lantana in various colors
fuchsias and German ivy
tuberous begonias, fancyleaf caladiums, crotons, Boston ferns,
and dusty miller
For hot, exposed locations, use the iceplant, *Mesembryanthemum crystallinum,* which has icelike crystals on the foliage.

References

Berrisford, J. 1975. *Window Box and Container Gardening.* Transatlantic
Arts, Inc., New York
Field, F. 1975. *Window Box Gardening.* Transatlantic Arts, Inc., New York
Gramenz, G. 1975. *Indoor Gardens and Window Boxes.* Intl. Pubns. Serv.,
New York
Teuscher, W. 1956. *Window-Box Gardening.* Macmillan Pub. Co., Inc.,
Riverside, N.J.

WINTER GREENS AND CHRISTMAS DECORATIONS

With a little imagination, nature can provide materials to
produce a great variety of simple, inexpensive Christmas decorations. Evergreen branches, cones, and seed pods can easily be
found and used to make wreaths, swags, tree ornaments, and
many other decorations.

Fresh greens should be collected either early or late in the
day. To condition the greens, place the cut stems in water and
place them in a cool, dark place for twenty-four hours. Long-

lasting greens are pine, cedar, yew, arborvitae, juniper, holly, and laurel. Avoid using hemlock, for it sheds its needles quickly. If cones are covered with pitch, place in a slow oven (100-200° F) to dry the pitch, and wash them if necessary.

Suggested Projects

Swags: Use two or three branches of greens either of the same variety or a mixture. Wire the branches together. Arrange the cones and seed pods, and decorate with a ribbon.

Garlands: Overlap and wire bunches of greens on a rope or heavy twine. Sweetgum fruits and small cones can be strung and sprayed to hang on the tree.

Wreaths: Wire bunches of greens to a circular wire form or to a styrofoam form with fern pins. Decorate with moss, cones, and berries.

Corsages: Mount various cones on a small circular piece of cardboard, and attach a pin.

A Miniature Christmas Tree

Select a potato that will fit into a 3-inch clay flower pot. Cut branches of spruce, fir, or any other small needled evergreen. Insert an 8 to 10-inch branch into the top of the potato standing straight up. Insert shorter branches at an angle starting at the center of the potato and working around the first branch. Work outward, using smaller branches and increasing the angle until the last row lies horizontal. Decorate the tree with tiny cones and ornaments, and gild the flower pot.

Topiary Tree

Use a Styrofoam ball, a dowel, greens (boxwood and false cypress), fern pins, container, and ribbon. Cover the entire ball with greens, using fern pins. Insert the dowel in the center of the ball and mount it in the container. Attach a ribbon.

ARTICHOKE CENTERPIECE

Artichokes may be dried in a sunny window. To give them a starburst effect, separate each leaf and insert a piece of cotton between them until they are completely dry. Arrange with greens and ribbon.

WALL TREE

Use a piece of Styrofoam that is 1 inch thick, lacy greens, fern pins, pine cones, fruit, and ribbon. Cut the Styrofoam into a tree shape. Start at the top, and arrange the greens with fern pins. Add other decorations.

SEED ORNAMENTS

Cover Styrofoam eggs with various seeds using silicone glue. Insert a hanger on the top.

FRAGRANCE TREE

Cover a Styrofoam cone with a piece of velvet or felt. Cut fancy net into 6-inch squares, fill each square with various spices, and secure them to the cone with a wired florist's pick. Use cinnamon sticks, whole cloves, ginger, orange peels, whole nutmeg, and allspice.

KITCHEN WREATH

Arrange one row of bay leaves to the outside of a Styrofoam ring. Attach another row pointing toward the center. Place a third row on top of these to fill in open spaces. Decorate with various herbs and spices.

PINE CONE SCALES

Strip the scales from a pine cone with pliers. Glue overlapping rows of scales onto Styrofoam cones or bells.

SEED FLOWERS

Cut cardboard discs (1/2 inch in diameter), and thread a piece of wire through the top and then down to form a stem. Glue on seeds starting from the outside edge. Arrange the seed flowers with greens in a container.

MANTEL MATCHES

Cover match boxes with contact paper. Make a small arrangement on the top with cone flowers, tiny acorns, and cone scales.

CONE TREE

Spray a Styrofoam cone with brown paint. Start at the base of the cone, and glue on larger cones first. After they are dry, fill in with smaller cones, seed pods, and nuts.

POMANDER BALL ARRANGEMENT

Pierce an orange, lemon, or lime with a fork and insert whole cloves. The fruit will harden as it dries. Place it in an arrangement with other greens and add a ribbon.

CONE ANIMALS

These are made by glueing together various parts of cones and pods, painting on eyes and adding bows for color. Tiny cones (hemlock) can be made into flying birds by adding two wings made from maple seeds and attaching a colorful feather for a tail. Larger cones can be made into owls. The base of the cone becomes the face with the stem as the beak. Attach eyes, cone scales for horns, and wire feet. Mount on a branch or piece of wood.

PINE CONE SANTA

Glue two pine cones together. Attach eyes, cotton, and a hat.

MISCELLANEOUS

Miniature dried gourds make attractive tree ornaments.

Spray pressed flowers of Queen Anne's lace with gold, silver, or other colors. Apply glitter, attach a string, and hang on the tree.

Arrange cones in a strawberry basket adorned with a ribbon.

Make mini-scenes in milkweed pods. Spray the outside with gold paint and line the inside with velvet. They may be set on a table or hung on the tree.

Spray sweetgum fruits with gold, silver, or white paint. Attach a piece of nylon thread through the top and hang it on the tree.

Decorate the tops of glass jars with small dried materials. Fill the jar with candy and nuts. These make wonderful gifts.

References

Goddard, H. S. 1967. *Gardener's Christmas Book.* Macmillan Pub. Co., Inc., Riverside, N.J.

McCay, J. B. 1972. *Create with Cones.* Great Outdoors Pub. Co., St. Petersburg, Fla.

Purdy, S. 1965. *Christmas Decoration for You and Me.* Lippincott, J. B., Co., New York

Chapter Eight

RESOURCE MATERIALS

BIBLIOGRAPHY

Horticulture — Therapy — Rehabilitation

Anonymous. 1966. "Rx for executive health: garden therapy." *Pop. Gard.* 17: 14-19.
———. 1969. "Handicapped among the flora and fauna." *Rehab. Rec.* 10: 20-21.
———. 1971. "Kansas State University offers new program in hort-therapy." *Flor. & Nur. Exch.* 155 (25): 15.
———. 1973. "Patient garden therapy program: The Burke Rehabilitation Center." *The Chronicle:* Autumn.
Barber, A. (unpublished paper). "Horticultural therapy." Menninger Memorial Hospital, Topeka, Kan.
Berkey, A. L. and W. E. Drake. 1972. *An Analysis of Tasks Performed in the Ornamental Horticulture Industry.* New York State College of Agriculture and Life Sciences, Cornell University, Ithaca, N.Y.
Black, B. 1971. "Horticultural therapy comes of age." *Gard. J.* 21(1): 8-11.
Brooks, H. and C. Oppenheim. 1973. *Horticulture as a Therapeutic Aid.* Monograph 49. Institute Of Rehabilitation Medicine, New York University Medical Center
Burlingame, A. W. 1959. "Gardening brings new hope and health." *Horticulture* 37: 482.
———. 1960. *Gardening Offered as a Therapy.* The Cornell Plantations, Ithaca, N.Y.
———. 1962. "Companion gardening." *Horticulture* 40: 455.
———. 1974. *Hoe for Health.* Alice W. Burlingame, 3891 Oakhills Drive, Birmingham, Mi. 48010
Bush-Brown, L. 1962. "Philadelphia's garden blocks and 4-H clubs." *Plants and Gard. N.S.* 18(2): 27.
———. 1969. *Garden Blocks for Urban America.* Charles Scribner's Sons, New York
Coe, S. M. 1973. "Hortitherapy: to teach the art of living." *Highland Highlights* Fall: 2-5. Highland Hospital, Asheville, N.C.
Conklin, E. 1972. "Plants serve basic human need." *Sou. Flor. & Nur.* 85(26): 19-21.
———. 1972. "Plants and flowers — fundamental essentials." *Landscape Ind.* 17(6): 28-29.

————. 1972. "Man and plants — a primal association." *Amer. Nur.* 136(9): 42.

Copus, E. 1972. "Career training in horticulture for handicapped young folks." *In* 1972 Yearbook of Agriculture, USDA 282-287.

Corning, M. E. 1960. "Here mental health grows through gardening." *Arboretum Leaves* 2: 20-22. Holden Arboretum, Cleveland, Oh.

Cotton, M. 1975. "Effectiveness of horticultural therapy in lowering aggressiveness of institutionalized delinquent adolescents." *NCTRH Lecture and Publication Series* 1(5): October.

Dennis, L., R. Halward, J. Lord, and A. S. White. 1975. *Proceedings of the Symposium — Horticulture as a Tool in Therapy.* Royal Botanical Gardens, Hamilton, Ontario

Draper, H. R. 1955. *Horticulture as Psychiatric Therapy.* Friends Hospital, Philadelphia, Pa.

Evans, O. 1976. "As their plants grow, so does their world." *New York Times,* July 11, p. 46.

Fitzjarrald, S. 1969. "Gardener's life after a heart attack." *Org. Gard. & Farm.* 16: 48-51.

Floyd, J. A. 1972. "Horticultural therapy." *Arbor. & Bot. Gard. Bull.* 6(2): 57.

Gilbreath, P. R. and A. P. Olson. 1976. "Hortitherapy van: design, equipment and use." *Research Series* No. 168. Hort. Dept. S.C. Agric. Expt. Sta., Clemson Univ., Clemson, S.C.

Gordon, F. 1961. "The forward look in garden therapy." *News of the Fed. Gar. Clubs of N.Y. State, Inc.* 33(1): 10.

Guspie, J. A. 1973. "How flowers help the handicapped." *Florist* 7: 42-43.

Hamilton, L., P. J. R. Nichols, and A. S. White. 1970. "Gardening for the disabled and elderly." *J. Roy. Hort. Soc.* 95(8): 358-369.

Hefley, P. D. 1973. "Horticulture: a therapeutic tool." *J. of Rehab.* 39(1): 27-29.

Hill, L. 1976. "Horticultural therapy discussed in Vermont." *Amer. Nur.* 144(11): 42, 44.

Hoffman, J. F. and C. E. Ervin. 1965. "Roses and rehabilitation." *Plants and Gard.* 21(2): 68-71.

Hunter, N. L. 1970. *Horticulture Programs in Prisons.* California State Polytechnic College, San Luis Obispo

Kaplan, R. 1973. "Some psychological benefits of gardening." *Environ. and Behavior* 5(2): 145-161.

Kiefer, I. 1975. "Melwood Center, gateway to independence." *Maryland:* summer.

Lees, C. B. 1970. *Gardens, Plants and Man.* Prentice-Hall, Englewood Cliffs, N.J.

Lemme, J. 1972. "Reformatory program teaches horticultural skills." *Amer. Nur.* 136(9): 62.

Leon, C. 1976. "Healing power of gardening." *House and Gard.* 148: 66-67.

Lewis, C. A. 1971. "Flowers on Avenue D." *Horticulture* 49: 30-31.

————. 1972. "Public housing gardens — landscapes for the soul." p. 277-282. *In* Landscapes for Living, USDA Yearbook of Agriculture, House Doc. 229.

————. 1973. "People-plant interaction." *Amer. Hort.* 52(2): 18-24.

Lowell, R. 1968. "A feeling for nature." *Rehab. Record* 9(1): 20-21.

Lubin, A. 1972. "Inner city neighborhood gardens create new community spirit." *In* Landscape for Living, USDA Yearbook of Agriculture, House Doc. 229, p. 275-277.

McCandliss, R. R. 1967. "The plants-man-the environment." Menninger Memorial Hospital, Topeka, Kan.

————. 1968. "Results of a survey on horticultural therapy." The Menninger Foundation, Topeka, Kan.

————. 1968. "A therapeutic arboretum." *Plants & Gard.* N.S. 23(4): 34-35.

————. 1969. "Horticultural therapy as a profession." American Horticultural Congress, Philadelphia, Pa.

————. 1972. "A career in horticultural therapy." *Menninger Perspective:* June-July.

McCann, L. 1961. "Adventure in garden therapy." *News of the Fed. Garden Clubs of N.Y. State, Inc.* 33(1): 11.

McCurry, E. 1963. "Flowers and gardens — therapy unlimited." Pontiac State Hospital, Pontiac, Mi.

McDonald, E. 1976. *Plants as Therapy.* Praeger Pubs., Inc., New York

Massingham, B. 1972. *Gardening for the Handicapped.* Shire Publs. Ltd. Aylesbury, Bucks, England

Menninger, C. F. 1942. "Philosophy about gardening." *Bull. Menn. Clinic* 6(3): 66.

Menninger, W. C. and J. F. Pratt. 1957. "The therapy of gardening." *Pop. Gard.* 8: 54.

National Easter Seal Society for Crippled Children and Adults. *The Wheelabout Garden.* Chicago, Ill.

Neese, R. 1959. "Prisoner's escape." *Flow. Gro.* 46: 39-40.

O'Conner, A. H. 1958. "Horticulture as a curative." *Cornell Plantation Bull.* 14(2): 42.

Odom, R. E. 1973. "Horticultural therapy: a new education program." *HortSci.* 8: 458-460.

Penwarden, E. 1967. *It's the Plants that Matter.* George Allen & Unwin, Ltd., London

Perry, M. 1968. "To beautify America: New York housing authority annual garden contest." *Home Gard.* 55: 42.

Prina, L. L. 1974. "Horticultural therapy." *New York Times,* March 10, p. 6.

Privette, C. V. *Greenhouse Designs for the Handicapped.* Cooperative Extension Service, Clemson Univ., Clemson, S.C.

Ross, S. 1973. *Plant Consciousness, Plant Care.* Quadrangle/The New York Times Co., New York

Salac, S. S., R. E. Neild, J. O. Young, and J. F. Merker. 1976. "Partners in horticulture therapy." *Amer. Nur.* 144(4): 14, 84-85.

Senn, T. L., A. R. Kingman, J. Sharpe, J. A. Hiott, W. Ballard, and W. Bell. 1974. "South Carolina's hortitherapy program: innovative development of individual potential through horticulture." *S.C. Agr. Exp. Sta. Dept. of Hort. Misc. Publ.* No. 10, Clemson Univ., Clemson, S.C.

Stainbrook, E. 1973. "Man's psychic needs for nature." *Nat. Parks and Conser. Mag.* 47(9): 22-23.

Stiney, C. 1959. "The patient garden at Carville Leprosarium." *Flow. Gro.* 46(7): 57-59.

Stone, E. H. 1971. "There's a wheelchair in the woods." *Parks and Recreation* 6(12): 18-21, 48-49.

Taloumis, G. 1966. "Horticultural therapy achieves results." *Horticulture* 44: 26-27.

Tartakoff, S. 1953. "Garden therapy." *Horticulture* 31: 256.

Tereshkovich, G. 1973. "Horticultural therapy: a review." *HortSci.* 8: 460-461.

Watson, D. P. 1966. "Therapy through horticulture." *Proc. 17th Inter. Hort. Cong.* 2: 191-193.

Watson, D. P. and A. W. Burlingame. 1960. *Therapy through Horticulture.* Macmillan Co., New York

Watson, D. P. and H. B. Tukey. 1953. "Horticulture as a therapy." *J. Roy. Hort. Soc.* 78(6): 202-208.

White, A. S., P. J. R. Nichols, R. Hay, F. Bach, M. Chaplin, B. Tyldesley, and P. H. Elliot. 1972. *The Easy Path to Gardening.* Reader's Digest Assoc. Ltd. and the Disabled Living Foundation, London

Gardening and Horticulture

Abraham, G. and K. Abraham. 1975. *Organic Gardening Under Glass.* Rodale Press, Inc., Emmaus, Pa.

Bailey, L. H. 1939. *The Standard Cyclopedia of Horticulture.* (3 vols.), The Macmillan Co., New York

Baker, J. 1972. *Plants are Like People.* Pocket Books, New York

Bayliss, M. 1975. *Plant Parenthood.* One Hund. One Prods., San Francisco, Ca.

Blake, C. L. 1972. *Greenhouse Gardening for Fun.* Wm. Morrow & Co., Inc., New York

Boy Scouts of America. 1971. *Gardening.* BSA, North Brunswick, N.J.

Carleton, R. M. 1971. *The Small Garden Book.* The Macmillan Co., New York

Casey, L. 1975. *Outdoor Gardening.* Lerner Pubns. Co., Minneapolis, Minn.

Crowe, S. 1958. *Garden Design.* Hearthside Press, Inc., New York

Cruso, T. 1969. *Making Things Grow: A Guide for the Indoor Gardener.* Alfred Knopf, Inc., Westminister, Md.

————. 1971. *Making Things Grow Outdoors*. Alfred Knopf, Inc., Westminister, Md.

Denisen, E. L. 1958. *Principles of Horticulture*. The Macmillan Co., New York

Dworkin, F. and S. Dworkin. 1974. *The Apartment Gardener: The Total Guide to Buying, Raising, and Living with Apartment Plants*. The New American Library, Inc., New York

Eaton, J. A. 1973. *Gardening Under Glass: An Illustrated Guide to Living with a Greenhouse*. Macmillan Pub. Co., Inc., New York

Edmond, J. B. et al. 1975. *Fundamentals of Horticulture*. McGraw-Hill Book Co., New York

Fenton, D. X. 1974. *Indoor Gardening*. Franklin Watts, Inc., New York

Foley, D. J. 1973. *Gardening: A Basic Guide*. Barnes & Noble, Inc., Scranton, Pa.

Forsberg, J. L. 1963. *Disease of Ornamental Plants*. Univ. of Ill., College of Agric. Special Pub. No. 3.

Foster, G. F. 1971. *Ferns to Know and Grow*. Hawthorn Books, Inc., New York

Franz, M. 1970. "City gardeners beat pollution and inflation." *Org. Gard. & Farm*. 17: 26-33.

Free, M. 1957. *Plant Propagation in Pictures*. Doubleday & Co., Inc., New York

Garner, R. J. 1958. *The Grafter's Handbook*. Oxford Univ. Press, New York

Geo. J. Ball, Inc. 1965. *The Ball Red Book* (11th ed.), West Chicago, Ill.

Gettings, T. 1974. "Things: designing your own garden tools." *Org. Gard. & Farm*. 21: 56-57.

Graf, A. B. 1974. *Exotica III — Pictorial Cyclopedia of Indoor Plants*. Charles Scribner's Sons, New York

Hammet, K. R. W. 1973. *Plant Propagation*. Drake Pubs., New York

Haring, E. 1967. *The Complete Book of Growing Plants from Seed*. Hawthorn Books, Inc., New York

Hartman, H. T. and D. E. Kester. 1975. *Plant Propagation: Principles and Practices*. Prentice-Hall, Englewood Cliffs, N.J.

Huxley, A. J. 1971. *Garden Terms Simplified*. Winchester Press, New York

James, J. 1964. *Create New Flowers and Plants — Indoor and Out*. Doubleday & Co., Inc., New York

Janick, J. 1972. *Horticultural Science*. W. H. Freeman & Co., San Francisco, Ca.

Kramer, J. 1973. *Gardening without Stress or Strain*. Charles Scribner's Sons, New York

————. 1973. *Grow Your Own Plants: From Seeds, Cuttings, Divisions, Layering, and Grafting*. Charles Scribner's Sons, New York

Link, D. and F. Stark. 1974. *Gardening for Beginners*. Bobbs-Merril Co., Inc., Indianapolis, In.

Loewer, H. P. 1974. *Bringing the Outdoors In: How to Do Wonders with*

Vines, Wildflowers, Ferns, Mosses, Bulbs, Grasses, and Dozens of Other Plants Most People Overlook. Walker and Co., New York

———. 1975. *Seeds and Cuttings: Plant Propagation Made Easy.* Walker and Co., New York

Mabe, R. E. 1973. *Gardening with Flowering House Plants.* Potpourri Press, Greensboro, N.C.

———. 1973. *Gardening with House Plants.* Potpourri Press, Greensboro, N.C.

McDonald, E. 1972. *The World Book of House Plants.* Popular Lib., New York

———. 1974. *Little Plants for Small Spaces.* Popular Lib., New York

Nehrling, A. and I. Nehrling. 1962. *Propagating House Plants for Amateur and Commercial Use.* Hearthside Press, Inc., New York

Nelson, K. S. 1966. *Flower and Plant Production in the Greenhouse.* Interstate Printers & Pubs., Inc., Danville, Ill.

Ortloff, H. S. and H. B. Raymore. 1962. *A Book About Soils for the Home Gardener.* M. Barrows & Co., Inc., New York

Poincelot, R. P. 1974. *Gardening Indoors with House Plants.* Rodale Press, Inc., Emmaus, Pa.

Powell, T. and B. Powell. 1975. *The Avant Gardener: A Handbook and Sourcebook of All That's New and Useful in Gardening.* Houghton Mifflin Co., Boston, Ma.

Pyenson, L. 1964. *Keep Your Garden Health.* E. P. Dutton & Co., Inc., New York

Reid, D. 1966. *Botany for the Gardner.* MacDonald & Co., London

Rockwell, F. F. and M. Free. 1953. *House Plants: Everyday Questions Answered by Experts.* Doubleday & Co., New York

Taylor, N. 1953. *Color in the Garden, Fragrance in the Garden.* D. Van Nostrand Co. Inc., New York

———. 1965. *The Guide to Garden Shrubs and Trees.* Houghton Mifflin Co., Boston, Ma.

Webber, R. 1968. *Early Horticulturists.* Kelly Pubs., Clifton, N.J.

Weiss, M. 1973. *201 Valuable Free Things for People Who Love Gardening.* The American Garden Guild, Garden City, New York

Westcott, C. 1950. *The Plant Doctor: The How, Why and When of Disease and Insect Control in Your Garden.* J. B. Lippincott Co., Philadelphia and New York

———. 1964. *The Gardener's Bug Book.* Doubleday & Co., New York

Wilson, L. 1972. *The Complete Gardener.* Hawthorn Books, Inc., New York

A LIST OF SELECTED AGENCIES, INSTITUTIONS, AND ORGANIZATIONS THAT HAVE ACTIVE PROGRAMS IN HORTICULTURAL THERAPY

Association for Retarded Children, Horticulture Training Program, 1000

Elmwood Avenue, Rochester, N.Y. 14620

Bancroft Community, Route 581, Mullica Hill, N.J. 08062

The Burke Rehabilitation Center, Patient Garden Therapy Program, 785 Mamaroneck Avenue, White Plains, N.Y. 10605

Cavalier Horticultural Training Center, 12 N. Sheppard Street, Richmond, Va. 23221

Charles Lea Center, Spartanburg, S.C. 29302

Clinton Valley Center, Horticultural Therapy Training Center, Pontiac, Mi. 48053

Cloves Lakes Nursing Home, 25 Fanning Street, Staten Island, N.Y. 10314

David Lokey Horticultural Center, Elkton, Md. 21921

Division of Youth Services of Florida State, Florida School for Boys at Okeechobee, Route 2, Box 250, Okeechobee, Fla. 33472

Easter Seal Rehabilitation Center of Southwestern Connecticut, 26 Palmers Hill Road, Stamford, Ct. 06902

Elmcrest Psychiatric Institute, 25 Marlborough Street, Portland, Ct. 06480

Flora Therapy, Inc., Garden Center of Greater Cincinnati, Cincinnati, Oh. 45215

Friends Hospital, Roosevelt Boulevard & Adams Avenue, Philadelphia, Pa. 19124

Essex County Hospital Center, Horticultural Therapy Program, Cedar Grove, N.J. 07009

Garden Center of Greater Cleveland, 11030 East Boulevard, Cleveland, Oh. 44106

Garden Clubs of America, 598 Madison Avenue, New York, N.Y. 10022

Heather Hill, Inc. P.O. Box 309, Chardon, Oh. 44024
(Senior citizens)

Henryton Hospital Center, Greenhouse Program, Henryton, Md. 21080

Highland Hospital, Asheville, N.C. 28801

The Holden Arboretum, Sperry Road, Mentor, Oh. 44060

Holmesview Center, Greenville, S.C. 29609

Institute of Rehabilitation Medicine, New York University Medical Center, 400 East 34th Street, New York, N.Y. 10016

Iowa Lakes Community College, Agricultural Education, Emmetsburg, Ia. 50536

Leary Educational Foundation, 7515 Lee Highway, Falls Church, Va. 22042

Lewis B. Puller Vocational Center, Inc., P.O. Box 306, Saluda, Va. 23149

Lincoln Veterans Administration Hospital, Lincoln, Neb. 68510

Mansfield Training School, Ornamental Horticulture Program, Mansfield, Ct. 06250

Massachusetts Correctional Institution, Bridgewater, Ma. 02324

Melwood Horticultural Training Center, Inc., 5606 Dower House Road, Upper Marlboro, Md. 20870

Menninger Foundation, Box 829, Horticultural Therapy Program, Topeka,

Kan. 66601

Milestone Therapeutic Community, Greenville, S.C. 29609

Morton Arboretum, Lisle, Ill. 60532

Mountain Comprehensive Care Center, 205 N. Arnold Avenue, Prestonsburg, Ky. 41653

National Council of State Garden Clubs, 4401 Magnolia Avenue, St. Louis, Mo. 63110

Nevile Greenery, Route 413, Newtown-Langhorne Roads, Newtown, Pa. 18940

New Hope Manor, Garrison, N.Y. 10524

New York Association for Retarded Children, Monroe County Chapter, 1000 Elmwood Avenue, Rochester, N.Y. 14620

Odyssey House Parents' Program, Horticultural Sciences, Ward's Island, New York, N.Y. 10035

Providence Center, 1790 Lincoln Drive, Annapolis, Md. 21401

Rhode Island Department of Corrections, Project "Mother Earth," 200 Sockanosset Crossroads, Cranston, R.I. 02920

Royal Botanical Gardens, Hamilton, Ontario, Canada L8N 3H8

Shoreline Training and Employment Services (STEM), Route 77, Guilford, Ct. 06437

Southeast Louisiana Hospital, P.O. Box 3850, Mandeville, La. 70448

Sunland Training Center, P.O. Box 852, Marianna, Fla. 32446

The University of Connecticut Bartlett Arboretum, 151 Brookdale Road, Stamford, Ct. 06903

Veterans Administration Hospital, Greenhouse Horticultural Therapy Program, 2200 Gage Boulevard, Topeka, Kan. 66622

Veterans Hospital, Marion, Ind. 46952

Vocational Rehabilitation Services, Citizen Advocates, Inc., Malone, N.Y. 12953

Whitten Village, Clinton, S.C. 29325

ORGANIZATIONS SPONSORING PROGRAMS IN GARDENING AND/OR HORTICULTURE

Boy Scouts of America, National Council, New Brunswick, N.J. 08903

Brooklyn Botanic Garden, Curator of Instruction, 1000 Washington Avenue, Brooklyn, N.Y. 11225

Camp Fire Girls, Inc., Program Development Department, 65 Worth Street, New York, N.Y. 10013

Children's Garden Project, Junior League of Brooklyn, Inc., 76 Montague Street, Brooklyn, N.Y. 11201

Cleveland Public Schools, Horticultural Education, Room 400, 1380 East 6th Street, Cleveland, Oh. 44114

4-H Clubs, U.S. Department of Agriculture, aided by state and county governments, and locally assisted through country extension services in all 50 states.

The Garden Club of America, 598 Madison Avenue, New York, N.Y. 10022

Horticultural Society of New York, 128 West 58th Street, New York, N.Y. 10012

Los Angeles County Department of Arboreta and Botanic Gardens, Arboretum P.O. Box 688, Arcadia 91006; Descanso Gardens, 1418 Descanso Drive, La Canada 91011; South Coast Botanic Gardens, 26701 Rolling Hills Road, Palos Verdes Peninsula 90274

Men's Garden Clubs of America, 5560 Merle Hay Road, Des Moines, Ia. 50323

National Council of State Garden Clubs, 4401 Magnolia Street, St. Louis, Mo. 63110

National Junior Horticultural Association, P.O. Box 603, North Amherst, Ma. 01059

National Parks Association, 1701 18th Street, N.W., Washington, D.C. 20009

National Youth Conference on Natural Beauty and Conservation, c/o Girl Scouts of the USA, 830 Third Avenue, New York, N.Y. 10022

New York Botanical Garden, Education Department, Bronx, N.Y. 10458

School Gardens Program, Board of Education, 131 Livingston Street, Brooklyn, N.Y. 11201

U.S. Department of Health, Education and Welfare, Office of Environmental Education, Office of Education, Washington, D.C. 20202

FILMS, FILMSTRIPS AND SLIDES

ABC Media Concepts, 1330 Avenue of the Americas, New York, N.Y. 10019

AIMS Instructional Media Services, Inc., P.O. Box 1010, Hollywood, Ca. 90028

American Documentary Films, 379 Bay Street, San Francisco, Ca. 90028

American Educational Films, 331 North Maple Drive, Beverly Hills, Ca. 90210

Churchill Films, 662 North Robertson Blvd., Los Angeles, Ca. 90069

Cinema Associate Productions, Inc., Box 621, East Lansing, Mi. 48323

Contemporary McGray-Hill Films, 828 Custer Avenue, Evanston, Ill. 60202

Encyclopedia Britannica Educational Corporation, 425 North Michigan Avenue, Chicago, Ill. 60621

Federated Garden Clubs of Conn. Inc., 396 Prospect Street, Wethersfield, Ct. 06109. "The Connecticut Garden Therapy Story" — a 74 slide program including script and cassette recording.

Holt, Rinehart and Winston, Inc., Media Department, 383 Madison Avenue, New York, N.Y. 10017

Index to Horticultural Films, American Horticultural Society, Mount Vernon, Va. 22121

Mass Media Associates, 2116 North Charles Street, Baltimore, Md. 21218
Michigan Department of Education, 735 East Michigan Avenue, Lansing, Mi. 48913
NBC Educational Enterprises, 30 Rockefeller Plaza, New York, N.Y. 10020
National Council for Therapy and Rehabilitation Through Horticulture, Mount Vernon, Va. 22121
Pan American Seed Co., P.O. Box 438, West Chicago, Ill. 60185
Pyramid Films, Box 1048, Santa Monica, Ca. 90406
Rodale Press Films, c/o Bullfrog Films, Box 114, Milford Square, Pa. 18935
Time-Life Films, 43 W. 16th Street, New York, N.Y. 10010
University of California, Extension Media Center, Berkeley, Ca. 94720
The University of Michigan Audiovisual Center, 416 Fourth Street, Ann Arbor, Mi. 48103
John Wiley and Sons, Inc., 605 3rd Ave., New York, N.Y. 10016

RECORDS AND TAPES

Bibliography of Garden Books for the Blind. Available in Braille and recorded forms. Division for the Blind and Physically Handicapped, The Library of Congress, 1291 Taylor Street, N.W., Washington, D.C. 20542. Request "Gardening for Blind Persons" by The Cleveland Society for the Blind.
Tapes for the Blind, 12007 South Paramount Blvd., Suite 2, Downey, Ca. 90242.

ASSOCIATIONS THAT DISSEMINATE INFORMATION TO THE PUBLIC INCLUDING PUBLICATION OF BOOKS AND PAMPHLETS; ALSO, A POSSIBLE SOURCE FOR ACTIVE GRANTS AND VOLUNTEERS

Alexander Graham Bell Association for the Deaf, Manager of Information Services, 3417 Volta Place, N.W., Washington, D.C. 20002
American Foundation for the Blind, 15 West 16th Street, New York, N.Y. 10011
American Horticultural Society, Mount Vernon, Va. 22121
American Organization for the Education of the Hearing Impaired, 1537 Thirty-fifth Street, N.W., Washington, D.C. 20007
American Printing House for the Blind (APH), 1839 Frankfort Avenue, P.O. Box 6085, Louisville, Ky. 40206
Association for Children with Learning Disabilities (ACLD), 5225 Grace Street, Pittsburgh, Pa. 15236
Association for Children with Retarded Mental Development, 902 Broadway, New York, N.Y. 10010

Association for Education of the Visually Handicapped, 1604 Spruce Street, Philadelphia, Pa. 19103

Braille Institute of America, 741 North Vermont Avenue, Los Angeles, Ca. 90029

Community Development Foundation, 345 East 46th Street, New York, N.Y. 10017

Council for Exceptional Children, 1920 Association Drive, Reston, Va. 22091

Division on Physically Handicapped, Homebound and Hospitalized Children (DOPHHH), c/o Council for Exceptional Children, 1920 Association Drive, Reston, Va. 22091

Easter Seal Research Foundation of the National Easter Seal Society for Crippled Children and Adults, 2023 W. Ogden Avenue, Chicago, Ill. 60612

Epilepsy Foundation of America, 1828 L Street, N.W., Suite 406, Washington, D.C. 20036

Foundation Center, 888 7th Avenue, New York, N.Y. 10017

4-H Program, Extension Service, U.S. Department of Agriculture, Washington, D.C. 20250

Garden Club of America, 598 Madison Avenue, New York, N.Y. 10022

ICD Rehabilitation and Research Center, 340 E. 24th Street, New York, N.Y. 10010

Instructional Materials Reference Center c/o American Printing House for the Blind, 1839 Frankfort Avenue, Louisville, Ky. 40206

International Society for Rehabilitation of the Disabled, 219 East 44th Street, New York, N.Y. 10017

Little City Foundation (Mentally Retarded), 185 N. Wabash Avenue, Room 1600, Chicago, Ill. 60601

Men's Garden Clubs of America, 5560 Merle Hay Road, Des Moines, Ia. 50323

National Amputation Foundation (NAF), 12-45 150th Street, Whitestone, N.Y. 11357

National Association for Mental Health, 1800 North Kent Street, Rosslyn, Va. 22209

National Association for Retarded Children (NARC), 2709 Avenue E, Arlington, Tex. 76011

National Association of the Physically Handicapped, 6473 Grandville Street, Detroit, Mi. 48228

National Braille Association, 85 Godwin Avenue, Midland Park, N.J. 07432

National Braille Press, 88 St. Stephen Street, Boston, Ma. 02115

National Committee for the Prevention of Alcoholism, 6830 Laurel Street, N.W., Washington, D.C. 20012

National Congress of Organizations of the Physically Handicapped, 7611 Oakland Avenue, Minneapolis, Minn. 55423

National Coordinating Council on Drug Education (NCCDE), 1211 Connecticut Avenue, Suite 212, Washington, D.C. 20036

National Council for Therapy and Rehabilitation through Horticulture,

Mount Vernon, Va. 22121

National Council of Senior Citizens, 1511 K Street, N.W., Washington, D.C. 20005

National Council of State Garden Clubs, 4401 Magnolia Avenue, St. Louis, Mo. 63110

National Council on Alcoholism, Two Park Avenue, New York, N.Y. 10016

National Council on the Aging, 1828 L Street, N.W., Washington, D.C. 20036

National Federation of the Blind, 218 Randolph Hotel, Des Moines, Ia. 30309

National Foundation for the Handicapped and Disabled, 1643 W. Ogden Avenue, Chicago, Ill. 60612

National 4-H Service Committee, 150 N. Wacker Drive, Chicago, Ill. 60606

National Junior Horticultural Association, c/o American Horticultural Society, Mount Vernon, Va. 22121

National Recreation and Park Association (NRPA), 1601 N. Kent Street, Arlington, Va. 22200

National Rehabilitation Association, 1522 K Street, N.W., Washington, D.C. 20005

National Society for Autistic Children (NSAC), c/o Ruth Dyer, 169 Tampa Avenue, Albany, N.Y. 12208

National Therapeutic Recreation Society, c/o National Recreation and Park Association, 1601 North Kent Street, Arlington, Va. 22209

Recording for the Blind, 215 East 58th Street, New York, N.Y. 10022

The Revitalization Corps, 1762 Main Street, Hartford, Ct. 06106

Sciences for the Blind, 221 Rock Hill Road, Bala-Cynwyd, Pa. 19004

United Way of America, 801 N. Fairfax Street, Alexandria, Va. 22314

Women's National Farm and Garden Association, c/o Mrs. Miles Nelson Clair, 17 Dorset Road, Waban, Ma. 02168

PROFESSIONAL JOURNALS AND NEWSLETTERS THAT PUBLISH ARTICLES CONCERNING THE DISABLED AND DISADVANTAGED

AABC Newsletter, Association for Advancement of Blind Children, 520 Fifth Avenue, New York, N.Y. 10036

Aging, U.S. Department of Health, Education and Welfare, Supt. of Documents, Govt. Printing Office, Washington, D.C. 20402

American Association of Nurserymen Newsletter, 835 Southern Building, Washington, D.C. 20402

American Education, U.S. Department of Health, Education, and Welfare, Office of Education, Supt. of Documents, Washington, D.C. 20402

American Foundation for the Blind Newsletter, American Foundation for the Blind Inc., 15 West 16th Street, New York, N.Y. 10011

American Journal of Occupational Therapy, American Occupational

Therapy Association, 6000 Executive Blvd., Suite 2000, Rockville, Md. 20852

American Occupational Therapy Association Newsletter, 251 Park Avenue South, New York, N.Y. 10010

American Society for Horticultural Sciences Newsletter, 615 Elm Street, St. Joseph, Mi. 49085

Association for Physical and Mental Rehabilitation Newsletter and Rehabilitation Brochures, Association for Physical and Mental Rehabilitation, 1265 Cherry Road, Memphis, Tn. 38117

Childhood Education, Association for Childhood Education International, 3615 Wisconsin Avenue, N.W., Washington, D.C. 20016

Deaf American, National Association of the Deaf, 5125 Radnor Road, Indianapolis, In. 46226

Dynamic Maturity, American Association of Retired Persons, 1909 K Street, N.W., Washington, D.C. 20036

Education and Training of the Mentally Retarded, Council for Exceptional Children, 1920 Association Drive, Reston, Va. 22091

Education of the Visually Handicapped, Association for Education of the Visually Handicapped, 919 Walnut Street, Philadelphia, Pa. 19107

Exceptional Children, Council for Exceptional Children, 1411 S. Jefferson Davis Highway, Suite 900, Jefferson Plaza, Arlington, Va. 22202

Florist Newsletter, National Research Bureau, 221 N. LaSalle Street, Chicago, Ill. 60601

Fountainhead Newsletter, American Association of Instructors of the Blind, 711 14th Street, N.W., Washington, D.C. 20005

Journal for Special Educators of the Mentally Retarded, American Association of Special Educators, 107-20 125th Street, Richmond Hill, N.J.

Journal of Gerontology, Gerontological Society, 1 DuPont Circle, Number 520, Washington, D.C. 20036

Journal of Rehabilitation, National Rehabilitation Association, 1522 K Street, N.W., Washington, D.C. 20005

Journal of Rehabilitation of the Deaf, Professional Rehabilitation Workers with the Deaf, Inc., 814 Thayer Avenue, Silver Spring, Md. 20910

Journal of the Handicapped Child, West Virginia Commission on Mental Retardation, Room 308, Embleton Building, Charleston, W.Va. 25301

Library for the Blind and Physically Handicapped Newsletter, Library for the Blind and Physically Handicapped, Georgia Dept. of Education, 1050 Murphy Avenue, S.W., Atlanta, Ga. 30310

Library for the Blind Newsletter, Milwaukee Public Library, Library for the Blind, Milwaukee, Wis. 53233

Men's Garden Clubs of America News, 5560 Merle Hay Road, Des Moines, Ia. 50023

MR/Mental Retardation, American Association on Mental Deficiency, 5201 Connecticut Avenue, N.W., Washington, D.C. 20015

National Association of the Physically Handicapped National Newsletter,

12614 Fiack Street, Silver Springs, Md. 20910

National Council on Alcoholism Newsletter, National Council on Alcoholism, 2 East 103rd Street, New York, N.Y. 10029

National Newsletter, National Association of Physical Therapists, 370 California Avenue, Suite M-1, West Covina, Ca. 91790

N.J.H.A. Newsletter, National Junior Horticultural Association, P.O. Box 603, North Amherst, Ma. 01059

NPF Newsletter, National Paraplegic Foundation, 333 North Michigan Avenue, Chicago, Ill. 60601

Paraplegia News, Paralyzed Veterans of America, Inc., 935 Coastline Drive, Seal Beach, Ca. 90740

Recording for the Blind Newsletter, 215 East 58th Street, New York, N.Y. 10022

Rehabilitation Literature, National Easter Seal Society for Crippled Children and Adults, 2023 West Ogden Avenue, Chicago, Ill. 60612

Rehabilitation News, Rehabilitation Internation USA, 20 West 40th Street, New York, N.Y. 10018

Rehabilitation Record, U.S. Rehabilitation Services Administration, Washington, D.C. 20201

Report of Education of the Disadvantaged, Capitol Publishers, Inc., Suite G-12, 2430 Pennsylvania Avenue, N.W., Washington, D.C. 20037

Retarded Adult, American Association of Special Educators, 107-20 125th Street, Richmond Hill, N.Y. 11419

Retirement Living, Harvest Years Publishing Co., Inc., 150 E. 58th Street, New York, N.Y. 10022

Science and Children, National Science Teachers Association, 1201 16th Street, N.W., Washington, D.C. 20036

Senior Citizens Today, 2530 J. Street, Suite 302, Sacramento, Ca. 95816

Special Children, American Association of Special Educators, 107-20 125th Street, Richmond Hill, N.Y. 11419

Special Teacher, New York State Association of Teachers of Mentally Retarded, 65 Court Street, 8th Floor, Brooklyn, N.Y. 11201

Teaching Exceptional Children, The Council for Exceptional Children, 1920 Association Drive, Reston, Va. 22091

Therapeutic Recreational Journal, National Therapeutic Recreation Society, 1601 N. Kent Street, Arlington, Va. 22209

Young Children, National Association for the Education of Young Children, 1834 Connecticut Avenue, N.W., Washington, D.C. 20009

PERIODICALS THAT DEAL WITH GARDENING AND HORTICULTURE

American Horticulturist, American Horticultural Society, Mount Vernon, Va. 22121

American Nurseryman, American Nurseryman Publishing Co., 343 S.

Dearborn Street, Chicago, Ill. 60604

American Society for Horticultural Science Journal, American Society for Horticultural Science, Box 109, 615 Elm Street, St. Joseph, Mi. 49085

Community Garden News, Suite G 17, American City Building, Columbia, Md. 21044

Cornell Plantations, Cornell University, 100 Judd Falls Road, Ithaca, N.Y. 14850

Florist, Florist's Transworld Delivery Association, 900 W. Lafayette, Detroit, Mi. 48226

Flower and Garden Magazine, Mid-American Publishing Corp., 4251 Pennsylvania Street, Kansas City, Mo. 64111

Flower News, Central Flower News, Inc., 549 W. Randolf Street, Chicago, Ill. 60606

Garden Club of America Bulletin, Garden Club of America, 598 Madison Ave., New York, N.Y. 10022

Garden Path (Ohio Association of Garden Clubs), Greenfield Publishing Co., 1025 N. Washington Street, Greenfield, Oh. 45123

Gardener, Men's Garden Clubs of America, 5560 Merle Hay Road, Des Moines, Ia. 50323

Horticultural Society of New York Bulletin, Horticultural Society of New York, Inc., 128 W. 58th Street, New York, N.Y. 10019

Horticulture, Massachusetts Horticulture Society, Horticulture Hall, 300 Massachusetts Avenue, Boston, Ma. 02115

National Gardener, National Council of State Garden Clubs, Inc., Magnolia Avenue, St. Louis, Mo. 63110

Organic Gardening and Farming, Rodale Press, 33 E. Minor Street, Emmaus, Pa. 18049

The Gardener, (published in Braille), c/o Miss K. Fleet, 48 Tolcarne Drive, Pinner, Middlesex, England HA 52 DQ

GENERAL SUPPLIES OF NURSERIES AND GREENHOUSES

Al Saffer Florist Supplies, 130 West 28th Street, New York, N.Y. 10010

A. M. Leonard & Son, Inc., P.O. Box 816, Piqua, Oh. 45356

Brighton By-Products Co., Box 23, New Brighton, Pa. 15066

Cassco, Box 550, Montgomery, Ala. 36101

Columbia Nursery Supply Co., P.O. Box 5068, Columbia, S.C.

E. C. Geiger, Harleysville, Pa. 19438

Florist Products, Inc., 1843 E. Oakton, Des Plaines, Ill.

Piedmont Garden Supply, Salisbury, N.C.

Slater Supply Company, Inc., 143 Allen Blvd., Farmingdale, N.Y. 11735; 730 West Main Street, Riverhead, N.Y. 11901; 416 South Cherry Street, Wallingford, Ct. 06492

Southern Agricultural Insecticides, Inc., Hendersonville, N.C. 28739
The Wetzel Seed Company, Inc., 128 W. Market Street, Harrisonburg, Va.
22801

Seed and Supplies

Asgrow Seed Co., Florida, N.Y. 10921; Mechanicsburg, Pa. 17055; Vineland,
N.J. 08360; Bradford, Ontario, Canada
George J. Ball, Inc., West Chicago, Ill. 60185
Bodger Seeds Ltd., Box 390, El Monte, Ca. 91734
Burgess Seed & Plant Co., P.O. Box 3000, Galesburg, Mi. 49053
W. Atlee Burpee Co., Philadelphia, Pa. 19132
Comstock Ferre & Co., 263 Main Street, Wethersfield, Ct. 06109
Denholm Seed Co., 222 North A Street, Lompoc, Ca. 93436
Ferry Morse Seed Co., Inc., P.O. Box 100, Mountain View, Ca. 94040
Raymond A. Fleck, Inc., Street Rd. (Route 132), Southampton, Pa. 18966
H. G. German Seeds, Inc., Smithport, Pa. 16749
Germania Seed Co., 6952 North California Avenue, Chicago, Ill. 60645
Gill Bros. Seed Co., Portland, Ore. 97216
Fred C. Gloeckner & Co., Inc., 15 East 26th Street, New York, N.Y. 10010
Goldsmith Seeds, Inc., P.O. Box 1347, Gilroy, Ca. 95020
Joseph Harris Co., Inc., Moreton Farm, Rochester, N.Y. 14624
Chas. C. Hart Seed Co., Wethersfield, Ct. 06109
Herbst Brothers Seedsmen Inc., 1000 N. Main Street, Brewster, N.Y. 10509
A. H. Hummert Seed Co., 2746 Chouteau Avenue, St. Louis, Mo. 63103
Jackson & Perkins Co., Medford, Ore. 97501
Henry F. Michell Co., King of Prussia, Pa. 19406
Olds Seeds, P.O. Box 1069, Madison, Wis. 53701
Pan-American Seed Co., Cortex, Fla.
George W. Park Seed Co., Inc., Greenwood, S.C. 29646
T. Sakata & Co., 2 Kiribatake, Kanagawa-Ku, Yokohama, Japan
Stokes Seeds Inc., Box 97, Buffalo, N.Y. 14201
Thompson & Morgan, (Ipswich) Ltd., Ipswich, England

Bulbs

Adamse-Lefeber, P.O. Box 583, Babylon, Long Island, N.Y. 11702
Dirk Visser & Co., P.O. Box 295 High Street, Ipswich, Ma. 01938
Dutch Gardens, Inc., P.O. Box 30, Lisse, Holland
French's Bulb Importer, P.O. Box 37, Lima, Pa. 19060
P. De Jager & Sons, Inc., South Hamilton, Ma. 01982
Oregon Bulb Farms, Gresham, Ore. 97030

Perennial Garden Flower Plants

Lamb Nurseries, E. 101 Sharp Avenue, Spokane, Wa. 99202
Martin Viette's Nurseries, Northern Boulevard (25A), East Norwich, Long
    Island, N.Y. 11732
Walter Marx Gardens, Boring, Ore. 97009
Wayside Gardens, Mentor, Oh. 44064
Weston Nurseries, East Main Street, Hopkinton, Ma. 01748
White Flower Farms, Litchfield, Ct. 06759
Sunny Border Nurseries, Kensington, Ct. 06037

Roses

Hand Rose Farms, Dallas Highway, Tyler, Tex. 75701
Jackson & Perkins, 1 Rose Lane, Medford, Ore. 97501
Somerset Rose Nursery, P.O. Box 608, New Brunswick, N.J. 08903
Star Roses, Conard-Pyle Co., West Grove, Pa. 19390

Garden Chrysanthemums

Stafford Conservatories, Stafford Springs, Ct. 06076
Star Mums, The Conard-Pyle Co., West Grove, Pa. 19390
Sunnyslope Gardens, 8638 Huntington Drive, San Gabriel, Ca. 91202
Thon's Garden Mums, 4815 Oak Street, Crystal Lake, Ill. 60014

Pansies

Harold's Seeds & Bulbs, P.O. Box 29-WZ, Grants Pass, Ore. 97526

Wild Flowers

Exeter Wild Flower Gardens, P.O. Box 510, Exeter, N.H. 03833
Gardens of the Blue Ridge, E. P. Robbins, Hardy Nature Plants, Ashford,
    McDowell County, N.C. 28603

Geraniums

Wilson Bros., Roachdale, In. 46172

Gladiolus

Jackson & Perkins Co., Medford, Ore. 97501
Knisley's Gladiolus Farm, Rural Route 1 Wichert Road, St. Anne, Ill.

Herbs, Oils and Spices

Caswell-Massey Co. Ltd., 320 West 13th Street, New York, N.Y. 10014
Fioretti Perfumes & Co., Inc., 1472 Lexington, Avenue, New York, N.Y. 10028
Kiehl Pharmacy Inc., 109 3rd Avenue, New York, N.Y. 10003
Paprikas-Weiss Importers, 1546 2nd Avenue, New York, N.Y. 10021

AT DAY'S END

Is anybody happier because you passed this way?
Does anyone remember that you spoke to him today?
The day is almost over, and its toiling time is through;
Is there anyone to utter now a kindly word of you?
Can you say tonight, in parting with the day that's slipping fast,
That you helped a single brother of the many that you passed?
Is a single heart rejoicing over what you did or said;
Does the man whose hopes were fading, now with courage look ahead?
Did you waste the day or lose it? Was it well or sorely spent?
Did you leave a trail of kindness, or a scar of discontent?
As you close your eyes in slumber, do you think that God will say,
"You have earned one more tomorrow by the work you did today"?

— John Hall

AUTHOR INDEX

215

SUBJECT INDEX

A

Acacia, 116
Achimenes, 101
Acorns, 126
Acti-dione PM, 111
African violets, 81, 82, 88, 96, 98, 103
Agave americana, 101
Aged, 47-49
Ageratum, 92
Aglaonema, 101
Agriform, 87
Air plants, 122
Alcoholics, 49-50
Alcoholics Anonymous, 50
Alders, 126
Aloe, 81, 101
Alum, 134
Aluminum, 85
Aluminum plant, 103
Amaryllis, 81
American Foundation for the Blind, 53
American Society of Landscape Artists, 20
Aminotriazole, 111
Andromeda, 116
Anemone, 99
Annuals, 94, 145
    cultivation for specific, 147
Anthurium, 101
Aphelandra, 101
Aphids, 109, 111, 112, 113
Apples, 40
Aqua-Grow, 81
Aralias, 99
    false, 102
Araucaria, 102
Arborvitae, 116
Artillery plant, 103
Asexual reproduction, 95
Asparagus, 102
Asparagus ferns, 95, 102

Asparagus juice, 112
Aspidistra, 95, 102
Ataxic, 68
Athetoid, 68
Avocado, 172
Azalea, 99, 116

B

Bacillus thuringiensis, 111, 112
Bark, 81
Bartlett Arboretum, 54
Basic H, 111
Baskets, hanging, 115, 166-168
    plants, suggested, 168-169
Bayberry, 126
Beans, 92
Beech, 116
Beechnuts, 126
Beets, 112
Begonia, 81, 82, 88, 92, 98, 101, 102
Beloperone, 102
Benlate 6, 111
Benomyl, 111
Berries, 126
Betasan, 111
Biennials, 145
Biofeedback, 10
Biotrol, 111, 112
Birch, 116
Birdseed, 172
Bittersweet, 126
Black leaf, 40, 110
Blind, 51-54
    gardens, 157-159
Blind Veterans Association, 53
Blood, dried, 85
Bloomington Garden Club (Indiana), 28
Bone meal, 85
Bonsai, 115, 116-118
Borax, 134